CW00734940

Shooting Sporting Clays

Mark Brannon and Tom Hanrahan

Shooting
Sporting Clays

With photo illustrations
by Matthew Brannon

Foreword by Anthony Matarese Jr.
National Sporting Clays Champion

STACKPOLE
BOOKS

Published by
STACKPOLE BOOKS
5067 Ritter Road
Mechanicsburg, PA 17055
www.stackpolebooks.com

Printed in China
First edition
10 9 8 7 6 5 4 3

Library of Congress Cataloging-in-Publication Data

Brannon, Mark.
    Shooting sporting clays / Mark Brannon and Tom Hanrahan ; with photo
illustrations by Matthew Brannon ; foreword by Anthony Matarese. — 1st ed.
       p.   cm.
    Includes index.
    ISBN-13: 978-0-8117-0618-6 (hardcover)
    ISBN-10: 0-8117-0618-4 (hardcover)
    1. Trapshooting.   I. Hanrahan, Tom.   II. Brannon, Matthew ill.   III. Title.
GV1181.B68   2011
799.3'132—dc22
                                               2010028378

To the gang at Arnold Trail

CONTENTS

s a professional shooting instructor and competitive sporting clays
shooter, I congratulate Tom and Mark for putting together such a
great book. This is the only book to my knowledge that explores
all facets of sporting clays. The complexity and dynamic of sporting
clays can be a bit overwhelming for new shooters, but this book will
surely help. The information and guidance will provide something for
shooters of all experience and skill levels.

The key to success in sporting clays lies in the development of fundamentals. This book walks the reader through the key fundamentals that
are necessary to lay the foundation for his or her shooting. Gaining a
proper understanding of stance, eye dominance, gun mount, break points,
hold points, FOCUS, and gun control is absolutely critical for shooters of
all levels. The fundamentals stressed throughout this book must be practiced
to develop the proper skills.

The development of key fundamentals and principles is not only necessary to become a proficient shooter, but specifically important to consistent performance. It will be particularly important to truly gain an
understanding that shooting a shotgun is about pointing, not aiming.
Learning to focus on the target and not your barrel is the most important thing you will ever learn. Remember, when you catch or hit a baseball, you watch the ball, not your glove or the bat.

Second only to focusing on the target is learning to have control of
the gun and developing a smooth swing. The authors do a great job
describing the correlation between hold points and being smooth. One

of the keys to consistent shooting is the ability to prevent the speed of the gun from deviating greatly from the speed of the target. In other words, you must understand how to match the speed of the gun to the speed of the target.

Whether you're a new shooter or a very experienced shooter, you will surely learn from this book. Remember, you must understand the fundamentals, have a plan, execute the plan, be consistent in every move, and practice to develop the fundamentals. Greatness is not born, it's grown, and this book will help you understand how.

> Anthony I. Matarese Jr.
> www.clayshootinginstruction.com
> 14-time NSCA All-American
> 2008 NSCA National Champion
> 2008 NSCA U.S. Open Champion
> 5 NSCA U.S. Open Podium Finishes
> 12 years' experience coaching

The trap launches, a target rockets across the sky, you shoulder your gun, and *pow!* The target turns to dust. Welcome to sporting clays, the world's fastest growing shooting sport. If you want to have fun with a shotgun, you've picked a wonderful and challenging game.

Sporting clays courses are laid out in the woods and open fields, with myriad setups in the field. The sport is played year-round, in rain and snow and bright sunshine. The shots are of an almost infinite variety and each course is an entirely different venue. Sporting clays is the closest thing to hunting real birds you will find outside of the forest in autumn. Every time you go to a tournament, the targets fly differently, making every tourney a unique experience. And the sport takes place in beautiful, pristine natural settings. What more could you ask of a sport?

This guide lays out the fundamentals of shooting clay targets. But it's also a story about perseverance, guts, and determination. No one has worked harder at learning to shoot than Tom Hanrahan. Ivy League educated, very smart, and not a little stubborn, he worked for years at shooting his way. He saw little improvement, but he has guts. He didn't quit; he was determined to improve.

Tom was lacking in good fundamentals, but he learned those fundamentals from Mark Brannon, one step at a time. And you can too.

Mark is a Master Class shooter in the National Sporting Clays Association and an NRA-certified shotgun instructor with many years' experience in teaching and competitive shooting. In his sporting clays career, he has had 40 first-place finishes in main events; he holds the L.L. Bean 5-Stand record with 62 perfect rounds in three years; he was selected for the 2009 and 2010 NSCA Zone 1 (Northeastern United States) All Star Teams. He has been helping shooters improve their games for nearly 20 years.

Mark observed early in his shooting career that the shooters who consistently scored the best paid the most attention to their form—how they set up for a shot and how they handled the gun. Foot position, hold point, focal point, break point, swing—mastery of these basic tenets of the game is what produces better scores.

In *Shooting Sporting Clays*, Tom and Mark share lessons learned along the way as Tom has made his way to B class. New shooters will learn the basics and intermediate shooters will pick up on important tips as they share Tom and Mark's journey toward better shooting.

Many books on shotgun shooting—and wing shooting—fail to teach the basics but focus instead on how to make a particular shot. This book aims to prepare a novice shooter for a leap forward in shooting success by emphasizing the fundamentals.

All the shooting fundamentals are covered in detail, from basic stance to advanced techniques for target-breaking success. This book will show you how to develop a plan and implement it, over and over again, until it is automatic.

Now Tom focuses on the fundamentals for each target, each and every time he steps into the cage. He has fully embraced the shooting fundamentals outlined within these chapters and his performance improvement has been dramatic.

Yours can be too.

Sporting Clays and Other Clay Target Sports

Sporting Clays

Sporting clays is the newest, hottest clay target shotgun sport in the United States. It is becoming wildly popular with people of all ages and income levels. Anyone with a shotgun can enjoy the sport, which combines many elements of trap and skeet, the two traditional American shotgun games, but goes far beyond those sports in its target diversity. Sporting clays is both a wonderful recreational opportunity at local gun clubs and a sophisticated competitive sport with a national tournament circuit, national champions, All-American teams, corporate endorsements, and a national sanctioning body.

Sporting clays has more in common with golf than it does with either trap or skeet—every golf course is unique as is every sporting clays course, but trap and skeet fields are the same worldwide.

More correctly known as English sporting clays, sporting clays began in Britain in the early twentieth century and, like trap and skeet, was designed to emulate bird hunting. It came to the United States in the 1980s and became a nationally organized sport in 1989 under the auspices of the

National Sporting Clays Association (NSCA). Of all the clay target sports, it most closely emulates bird hunting in the variety of shots available, but it has taken target trajectories far beyond what any flesh and blood bird can do.

It's normally shot with a 12-gauge shotgun, and like trap and skeet, uses the standard, 108-millimeter target (among others), but that's where the similarities with trap and skeet end. There's nothing regimented or predictable about the game or its derivatives, 5-stand and FITASC (pronounced fee'-task).

A sporting clays course usually consists of a hundred targets shot at from 10 to 16 stations. Each station consists of two separate target presentations with a shooting menu that describes the number of targets and how they will be shot. The presentations can be almost any targets imaginable: One target might be a fast crosser, the other a straight-up teal. Or one a rabbit target running on the ground with the second target a low, slow, fading quartering incomer. Only the target setter's imagination limits the possible target presentations. Target sequences can be singles (two shots allowed); a report pair, where the first target is launched within three seconds of the shooter's call and the second launched when the shooter fires at the first target; or true simultaneous pairs, where both targets are launched at the same time. Then there is the following pair, typically two targets from the same trap thrown as fast as the trap can cycle. A single station's eight-target menu could encompass all four types of target sequences. Station menus vary from shoot to shoot even at the same club. One station menu may call for a single target from each trap and then three report pairs. The very next station could call for four simultaneous pairs—no singles or report pairs at all. There are very few rules in sporting clays defining how targets should be set or in what sequence they should be fired on. As a result, the variety is endless.

5-Stand and FITASC

Of the two derivative games mentioned earlier, 5-stand and FITASC, 5-stand is much more popular and is shot recreationally at many locations—even at clubs that don't hold competitive tournaments. Sporting clays shooters often practice with 5-stand when they can't get onto a sporting clays course.

An abbreviated version of sporting clays, 5-stand offers the same varied target presentations as sporting clays. The game has several different skill levels and uses six or eight automatic traps to simulate game birds.

A typical portable sporting station. The cage and traps are moveable and can be positioned almost anywhere.

Targets are released in a predetermined set sequence marked on a menu card in front of each shooting station.

The game consists of five separate shooting stations, or cages, not more than 4 1/2 feet wide and set about 15 feet apart center-to-center. These cages are designed for safety, the same way they are on sporting clays courses, forming a window that prevents excessive gun movement.

The cages are spread out in a straight line. The first shooter fires first every round for a total of 25 targets thrown as singles, report pairs, and simultaneous pairs thrown in succession. After each shooter has fired 5 times, all shooters rotate to the next cage in line, ensuring the maximum number of angles to the targets. The effect of these changing target angles is that no two targets are ever the same for each shooter. The shooter will fire on what amounts to 25 unique targets.

The game of 5-stand offers a lively sporting clays course within stricter geographical boundaries than are normally found on a traditional course. At many top venues, the 5-stand competition is as earnestly contested as the sporting clays course.

FITASC (Fédération Internationale de Tir aux Armes Sportives de Chasse), also referred to as International Sporting or Parcours de Chasse Sporting, is similar to 5-stand. While the NSCA is the sole sanctioning authority within the United States, FITASC is an international body with headquarters in Paris, France. It is the form of sporting clays used in international competition.

A portable 5-stand setup on a skeet field. Note the menus in holders in front of the cages.

A shooter swings on a FITASC target. Our parcours is set up on an old skeet field. Note the traps behind her below the skeet high house.

In FITASC, you shoot 25 targets in a predefined shooting area of about 40 yards by 40 yards, called a parcour. Each parcour uses 3 to 5 traps and multiple shooting stations, called pegs. A competitive FITASC event could have 50 to 100 targets, using one parcour for each 25 targets. FITASC has many rules regarding gun mount, dress code, and etiquette. It is becoming increasingly popular as a side event at large NSCA sporting clays tournaments. It is considered the most difficult of all the sporting clays events because of the target distances and technical presentations.

Sporting Targets

There are almost no rules for how to set a target. The only limitations on target presentation are safety and the imagination of the target setter. Targets can be arching over your head, bouncing on the ground, popping up behind a tall tree and then falling to the ground, or thrown diagonally into the ground from a trap set up on a 100-foot-tall tower. And all from 5 to 75 yards away!

Then you have targets that are quartering away and quartering in, the long crossers, the fading droppers right at your feet. Trap machines for

A portable sporting station set up on a trap field uses an old Winchester skeet machine for a 2-target presentation.

sporting clays have tilt adjusters, so even a target thrown in a straight line doesn't stay that way for long. It curls as it flies, causing interesting visual effects that make it tricky to hit, especially when combined with changes in terrain like slopes or gullies.

The variety of target presentations is unlimited and ever-changing. And that's just for the 108-millimeter target. There are also midi, mini, battue, and rabbit targets, each with unique flight characteristics.

The midi (mid-sized) target is the same shape but smaller than the standard target at 90 millimeters. Because of its lighter weight, it leaves the trap machines much faster than a standard target, but it slows down much faster than the standard target, too. It also looks like it is farther away than a standard target at the same distance. The midi target makes life much more interesting for the sporting clays shooter.

The mini target, short for miniature, is only 60 millimeters in size but otherwise similar to the standard and midi in construction. Because of its small size and light weight, it flies incredibly fast off the trap and can be very difficult to see. At anything past 25 yards, it looks like a tiny dot flying in the air.

The three basic targets used in sporting clays. From left: the 108-millimeter standard, 90-millimeter midi, and the 60-millimeter mini.

The rabbit (left) and battue targets. Both are the same diameter as the standard target, but the battue is very thin and fragile with almost no dome, while the rabbit target is thick and tough enough to bounce on the ground without breaking.

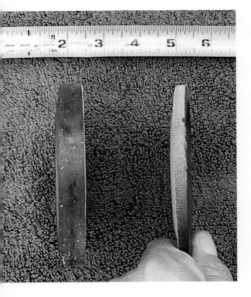

The rabbit (left) and battue targets on edge. Note the difference in thickness.

The battue is a target many shooters curse with enthusiasm. It is the same size as a standard target, but it has almost no dome—it's a 108-millimeter nearly flat disk. It's generally thrown as a high target, but when it begins to fall it rolls over and drops on edge with the flight characteristics of a boulder. It is nearly invisible when it's rising and can only be seen clearly after it rolls over and begins to drop, showing its face to the shooter. Some inventive target setters stack their battue traps with alternating targets—one right side up and one upside down—and throw the targets as a following pair. The results are two distinctly different and hard-to-hit targets from the same machine.

The rabbit target is a heavy, reinforced, flat clay disk designed to bounce on the ground at high speed and not break. Because of its construction, it is hard to break with tiny shotgun pellets. You need lots of choke and the heaviest shell you own for the rabbit target.

A rabbit target can be either thrown on the ground or in the air. One thrown in the air flies like a rock—and breaks about as hard as one too. When thrown on the ground, it slows down very fast and gives even experienced shooters grief. Luckily, it is the only target type to move that way. On the ground, it presents an optical illusion because it is in contact with its background (the ground), which leads a shooter to believe it is faster than it actually is. The shooter over-leads the target, missing in front. To add insult to injury, after a shooter fires and misses, when he recovers from the recoil and see the still-rolling rabbit, it's rolled through the dust cloud caused by his shot, convincing him that he missed behind. On his next shot, he shoots even farther in front, missing again.

Sporting clays is a far more difficult sport than either trap or skeet. It requires that you know how to break a wider variety of targets under infinitely variable speeds and distances. You must master the use of chokes and ammo to squeeze every bit of performance from your shotgun that you

Shooting partner Bub Copp swings on a rabbit target. Rabbits roll on the ground and appear faster than they are, making them difficult to hit.

Mark hammers a rabbit. Unexpected bounces are the norm for the rabbit target. Stare hard at the target and let your hands move the gun subconsciously to ensure a hit.

TOM'S TAKE   Skeet was my initiation to clay targets, as it is for many others. Skeet is a great game, consisting of a highly regimented set of targets—pretty much the same targets over and over again. It's a lot less varied than sporting clays.

I took up trap—a game with the same highly regimented targets, except the targets were all going away—some time later. It too is a lot less varied than sporting clays. When I began to shoot sporting clays, I found that it was entirely different: targets I had never seen before, targets I had never even imagined! Targets from above and behind and crossing and falling and curling and curving. . . . And each course was different, every tournament a different world of presentations.

I was hooked, completely and utterly captivated. Sporting clays was a game that really was like hunting birds in the woods. Mark told me I would never shoot the same course twice if I traveled from one tournament to the next. How do you get bored shooting a game like that?

I met a lot of shooters who had moved from skeet and trap for the very same reasons I had—to shoot a more complex and challenging discipline with an infinite variety of targets. I wondered: Should I shoot trap and skeet or just concentrate on sporting clays exclusively? Am I too jaded about repetitive target presentations? Skeet and trap are games of perfection. If you miss a single target in a competition, you are more or less out of it. I think this is why skeet and trap shooters are so high-strung—because they go crazy if they miss a single target.

can. Sporting clays pushes the envelope of what a shotgun can do. No other clay target sport makes such demands of the shooter and equipment.

All this sounds intimidating if you are a novice shooter, but it need not be. There is nothing magical or otherworldly about breaking a clay target with a shotgun. At its essence, successful shotgunning is a series of mechanical functions combined with eye and hand coordination, refined with practice. Anyone can do it, and do it very well with sufficient practice. And keep in mind that if you do decide to enter competitions, even as a novice, you will only be competing against shooters of similar abilities.

The following chapters break down the mechanical functions and teach you how to master them. By incorporating them into your shoot-

Trap is more fun for me than skeet because in trap you are never exactly sure where the target is going to go—just that it is going to be going away. Skeet is so static! You never step onto a skeet range and say, "Wow, did you see that high 5? What a cool target!" because high 5 is always the same. Skeet shooters are groove shooters because they know the target is always the same at every station.

There is a feeling in the shooting community that good sporting clays shooters can shoot any game, but that good trap or skeet shots do not necessarily do well at sporting clays because they are not accustomed to widely varying and unexpected presentations.

I like 5-stand, the compact version of sporting clays, much better than trap or skeet, because 5-stand has a variety of target presentations and a level of difficulty beyond what skeet and trap offer. Still, it is not as completely dynamic in its presentations as sporting clays. However, practically speaking, 5-stand is sporting clays on a more structured course. You still have a wide range of target presentations.

When I go to the range, if for some reason I cannot shoot sporting clays and have to shoot skeet or trap, I am instantly deflated. I'll shoot a round or two of each, but then I become bored. I want to see different targets doing different things. I want to be challenged!

So of what value is shooting skeet or trap to the dedicated sporting clays shooter?

ing game, you will save time and countless rounds downrange as you learn to shoot.

Sporting clays is not a game of perfection. Shooters have achieved perfect scores, but they are very, very rare. At the 2007 Lobster Classic at Addieville, Rhode Island, the undisputed world's best sporting clays shooter, Sir George Digweed, MBE and fifteen-time world English sporting champion, won the shoot with a 95.5 percent. That's far from perfection, and he's the best in the world! Everyone misses at sporting clays.

So how is it possible to master every type of target presentation? How do you break targets you've never even seen before, let alone practiced? You break those targets by applying the basic shooting principles

outlined in the following chapters, and by practicing until those principles are automatic.

Trap

Trap is the oldest of the three clay target games in the United States. It was
introduced about one hundred years ago and was originally intended as an
aid to the upland bird shooter. The sanctioning authority for trap in the
United States is the American Trap Association (ATA).

There are three basic events within sanctioned competitive trap: 16-
yard trap, handicap trap, and trap doubles.

A sanctioned trap field has five shooting pads 3 yards apart, laid out in
a semicircle and positioned 16 yards behind the target-throwing machine.
The trap machine is housed below grade in a low building and throws
targets out and slightly up at about 40 miles per hour. The machine sits on
an oscillating base that randomly moves through a 34-degree arc—17
degrees on each side of center line. Behind each of the five trap shooting
stations are 11 yardage markers for handicap trap.

Handicap trap is a method for increasing the difficulty of the shot by
increasing the distance the shooter stands behind the target-throwing
machine. In doubles trap, two targets are thrown simultaneously with the
oscillator turned off and the shooter at the 16- (closest) yard line.

All three forms of trap use the standard, 108-millimeter dome target,
usually painted orange.

An experienced trap shooter will break the target between 15 and
20 yards from the trap machine, making a roughly 30- to 35-yard shot
from the 16-yard line and up to a 50-yard shot from the 27-yard handicap line.

Trap is anything but an easy game. But the equipment and instruction
are so good that shooters need near-perfect scores to win. Add to that the
repetitive nature of the targets—they're all going-away targets—and you
have a game of intense focus and concentration. Not that sporting clays
does not require focus, but trap requires unremitting concentration
through the entire round. Sporting clays requires such concentration only
within the shooting box and in preparation for a station.

Virtually all competitive trap shooters use a come-from-behind swing
to break the target, much like bird hunting. They do this for two reasons:
first, they never know where the target is going because of the oscillator;

and second, a trap target doesn't travel horizontally or vertically enough in relation to the shooter to allow a maintained-lead or pull-away swing, which we'll talk about more in later chapters. Those styles would result in a dead-gun or poke shot and a sure miss. Trap requires finesse—this is especially true in handicap trap where, due to the distances, very little perceived lead is required.

Sporting clays has many trap-like targets, making trap perfect practice for learning how to control your gun in a swing-through situation that requires finesse. If your club allows it, turning the oscillator off and standing to the right and left of the stations is also very valuable practice for sporting clays as these target presentations are very common.

American Skeet

Skeet, like trap, has been around a long time. Started in the 1930s, skeet also began as a sport designed to improve bird-hunting skills but quickly matured into a target sport in its own right. The sanctioning authority for American skeet is the National Skeet Shooting Association (NSSA). Although participation in competitive skeet has dropped significantly in the last decade, it is still very popular as a noncompetitive sport for tens of thousands of shooters at small clubs all over the country.

In skeet, two traps are set about 40 yards apart with eight fixed shooting stations. On a clock face, the high house trap is at 9 o'clock and the low house trap is at 3 o'clock. Each trap throws a standard, 108-millimeter domed target at about 50 miles per hour roughly toward the other trap (with a slight outward angle so the target doesn't actually hit the other trap house but passes downrange of it). The target trajectory and speed is strictly regulated by the NSSA and must be consistent within inches to be a legal tournament target. Stations 1 through 7 are in a half-circle evenly spaced through the bottom of the clock face. (Station 4 is at 6 o'clock.) In the center of the field, equal distance from both houses and located in the center of the clock, is station 8. Targets are fired at in sequence starting from station 1 and include a combination of singles and doubles (depending on the station) for a total of 25 shots.

Skeet is excellent practice for sporting clays. We refer to it as "shotgun boot camp" because it encompasses many of the basic target presentations seen in sporting clays, but the targets are usually much closer (and therefore more forgiving of mistakes and easier to break).

Not all traps are fancy and new! This old Winchester skeet trap has served shooters for over 40 years.

At the competitive level, skeet, like trap, is a game of perfection. At anything other than a small local tournament, perfect scores are required to win.

Skeet tournaments consist of five basic events. Whereas handicap trap changes distances to increase the difficulty level, skeet uses smaller gauges to achieve the same result. Basic skeet events include 12-, 20-, 28-gauge and .410 bore shotguns shooting a combination of singles and doubles targets. The skeet doubles event is usually shot with a 12-gauge gun and includes only true pairs from stations 1 through 7.

Virtually all competitive skeet shooters shoot everything on a skeet field as maintained (or sustained) lead. This works well because the target trajectory is known (unlike trap), and because most targets travel horizontally in relation to the shooter. Most important for high scores, sustained lead is easy to duplicate because its basis is the target's own speed and the speed never changes.

Because skeet is a game of perfection, much emphasis is placed on shooting form in the competitive skeet community. The skeet field is a perfect place to practice good form. Because there are no mysteries to solve with the targets, all your emphasis can be on the shooting basics: head on the gun, feet positioned correctly, good hold points and target pickup points, solid follow-through.

Also, you can practice many sporting clays target presentations on a skeet field. Fast quartering-away targets, for example, give many people

TOM'S TAKE I don't like to see the same target presentations repeatedly, like in trap or skeet. Both are games of perfection in which the same targets are thrown over and over, and you must master a very particular set of targets. To be competitive you have to post a perfect score. On the sporting clays course, we have a rollicking good time, and nobody expects to post a perfect score. I think not being able to score a perfect score helps everyone relax.

I think skeet and trap are helpful games to improve your fundamental skills with a gun. Mark taught me that skeet is the best game for learning how to insert into the lead and shoot sustained lead. And every sporting clays course features trap-like going-away targets. So what better place to practice those targets than on a trap course?

Mark says every shooter should learn how to shoot skeet and trap, and he is right. One of the things that really helped him excel in sporting clays is that he was able to visualize many targets in relation to a skeet target. Why is it that many good skeet and trap shots cannot move easily to sporting clays but that many good sporting clays shooters can easily master skeet and trap? I think it is because sporting clays shooters have a broad repertoire of shots and can easily adjust to any given game. Shooters used to repetitive targets are easily flummoxed when the target presentations prove more diverse.

Mark has taught me to fear no game and be willing to try anything and everything with a shotgun. Try FITASC. Do it all. Otherwise, you will never become an all-around shot, and all-around shots make the best sporting clays shooters. The more games you try, the better you become at different shots.

fits. Quartering targets on stations 2 high and 6 low are as fast as you'll ever see on a sporting clays course. Then there's driven target practice on station 8 and overhead going-away targets on station high 1. If your club allows it, a skeet field is a perfect place to practice long fast crossers from behind station 4.

At our home club in Sidney, Maine, we have an extra-long skeet pull cord so we can get 30 yards behind any of the stations. If you want to learn to shoot a 50-yard rocket quartering-away target, stand 30 yards behind station 6 and call for a bird. A skeet field with a long cord is a perfect place to practice.

Shotguns

Almost any off-the-shelf shotgun capable of firing two shots will be adequate to get you started shooting sporting clays. Inexpensive side-by-sides, pump guns, and autoloaders are common sights on any sporting clays course. When you're ready to upgrade to a sporting clays-specific shotgun, there are many available in all price ranges. All of the major U.S. gunmakers and most European gunmakers make a shotgun specifically configured for the sport. These are usually more expensive than general-purpose field shotguns, sometimes much more so. Sporting clays guns often have a longer, higher adjustable stock or comb appropriate for target guns, and they usually have a longer barrel than a field gun. Many sporting clays guns are made from a higher grade of wood with a better finish. Many also include engraving on the receiver. Although more attractive wood and fancy engraving aren't required for sporting clays, they enhance the gun's appearance and are popular options.

Sporting clays-specific guns come primarily in two types: autoloaders and over-and-unders. Autoloaders are usually less expensive than over-and-under shotguns because they are not built to the same exacting tolerances. A quality over-and-under shotgun is precision-built to last a lifetime. An autoloader is by comparison more prone to breakdowns. American and European gunmakers manufacture a wide selection of sporting clays specific shotguns that range in price from $1,000 to $10,000 for standard models and over $100,000 for extra-fancy wood and custom engraving. We won't presume to tell you which is the best gun for sporting clays. That's a decision only you can make based on your budget and tastes. We will tell you what characteristics we believe a good sporting clays gun should have.

Whether you choose a pump gun, autoloader, side-by-side, or over-and-under, it should be the right weight, balance, and fit for you. We recommend a 12-gauge gun for everyone except those weighing less than 100 pounds, who will be better suited with a 20 gauge.

Bub and his beautiful Crown grade K-80. One of the joys of the sport is today's many glorious shotguns, from the relatively inexpensive to the very expensive custom grades that all the manufacturers produce.

Sporting clays is a game of instinct far more so than other clay target sports. The gun must become an extension of you, and you must be able to move instinctively with it without conscious thought. Often while you are shooting sporting clays, things happen so fast conscious thought and decision-making are impossible. You see, you move, you shoot—all sub-consciously. You must be able to move the gun quickly and smoothly with full control at all times, and the gun must shoot where you point it. For this to happen, the gun must fit you and its weight and balance must be right for your build.

If the gun is too heavy for your build or out of balance, much thought and effort will be required to get it to where it needs to be—it will not move naturally. You'll find yourself shoving it into position and consistently missing targets.

Gun Fit

Gun fit is a more important issue for sporting clays than in either trap or skeet. In those sports, the gun is fully mounted before calling for the target. This gives the shooter an opportunity to fit himself into the gun by moving the gun up or down on his shoulder or moving his head to achieve the correct eye/rib alignment. In sporting clays, the gun should not be fully mounted when calling for the target except for a few types of targets. To do so obstructs vision too much for a sport where targets could be coming from anywhere. This means the gun must fit perfectly when mounting without the shooter checking bead alignment and fitting himself to the gun. In this section we'll show you how to check your shotgun to ensure a proper fit.

Many target guns are capable of various adjustments to ensure fit, and if necessary, a professional stock fitter can ensure a perfect fit.

As your right eye is the rear sight on a shotgun (or left eye for left-handed shooters), your head must be correctly positioned on the stock when the gun is mounted for the gun to shoot where you point it. Your right eye must be perfectly centered on the rib at exactly the same height as the rib. You should not have to jam your face into the stock to achieve correct alignment. Nor should you see the back of the receiver with only light face-to-wood contact.

If your eye is positioned too high, the gun will shoot high. Too low and the gun will shoot low and you will severely obstruct your vision. If your eye does not line up correctly, there are a number of options, such as adjustable stocks, adjustable combs, or stock bending or cutting.

Above left: *Correct eye alignment as seen from the target's point of view.* Above right: *A closeup of rib alignment from the shooter's point of view with the gun fully mounted and light pressure between the gun's comb and the shooter's cheek.* Left: *Note the distance between the mid-bead and the end bead. This is the view over the rib if the stock is set too high for sporting clays. This is more typical of a trap gun sight picture.*

You should have approximately a 2-inch gap between your rear hand (on the gun's wrist) and your nose when the gun is mounted so that your thumb will not jam into your nose or glasses when the gun fires and recoils. This gap can be adjusted by lengthening or shortening your stock. Some autoloaders come with recoil pads of various thicknesses for just this reason. Otherwise this is done with shims behind the recoil pad to lengthen the stock or by cutting narrow strips off the rear of the stock to shorten it. Most gunsmiths can easily do either of these tasks.

The recoil pad should fit flush with your shoulder when the gun is mounted so that the force of recoil is distributed over the widest possible surface area. If the recoil pad only contacts your shoulder in one small area, the force of recoil is greatly magnified. An incorrectly fit shotgun kicks harder than one properly fitted to you.

Left: *Correct stock fit. Note the distance between the heel of George's right thumb on the gun's wrist and his nose—about 2 inches. Just right.* **Right:** *A stock too short for the shooter. Note how close Bub's nose is to his right thumb. When the gun recoils, the heel of his right thumb is pushed into his face and glasses—sometimes violently, depending on his ammo.*

Pitch is the angle of the recoil pad in relation to the barrel's rib. A neutral pitch (one that pitches the gun neither up nor down) is exactly perpendicular to the rib. Up-pitch has a positive angle in relation to the rib, while down-pitch has a negative angle. We believe that a mostly down pitched recoil pad is best for most sporting clays shooters because so many targets are dropping targets.

To quickly measure pitch, place your gun's recoil pad on the floor near a doorjamb. Make sure the recoil pad is flush with the floor and not rocked up at either end. Now gently slide the gun up to the doorjamb, keeping the recoil pad perfectly flush with the floor so that the comb of the stock or the receiver touches the doorjamb. If the barrel touches the jamb, you have upward pitch. You can measure how far the stock comb is from the wall and compare that measurement to another gun. If the comb or receiver touches the doorjamb, you have either neutral or down-pitch. If your barrel lies flush with the doorjamb, you have neutral pitch. If the end of the barrel stands out from the doorjamb, you have down-pitch.

Left: *To measure pitch using a doorjamb, position the gun so the recoil pad is flush with the floor and the receiver is against the doorjamb.* **Top right:** *One-inch down pitch on the standard Krieghoff sporting stock.* **Bottom right:** *Almost six inches of down pitch with the 391 Urika 2.*

A gun with down-pitch directs recoil backward instead of back and upward, and the down-pitch dramatically changes how easily the gun swings down on a dropping target.

The purpose of up- or down-pitch on a recoil pad is to ensure a flush fit between your shoulder and the recoil pad in order to evenly distribute recoil.

How to Check Gun Mount and Fit

You can do a simple and effective test of your gun fit and the consistency of your mount. It requires a 5-by-5-foot flat board and white and black spray paint.

First, cover the entire board with white paint. Then paint four to six 4-inch targets on the board, equal distances apart.

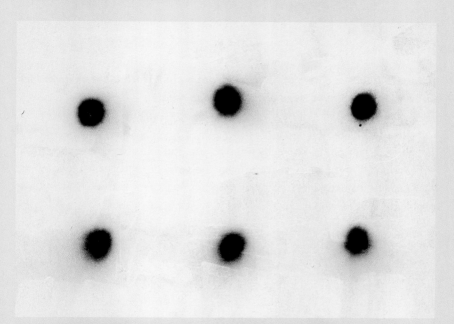

A board like this 5-by-5-foot steel plate with black targets can be used to test your gun fit and the consistency of your mount.

Use your favorite shell and fairly tight chokes (light-modified or modified). Set up about 25 yards from the board, observing all safety precautions. Take your stance as though you were preparing to shoot a clay target. Stare at only the black target on the board. Without taking your eyes off the target, mount and shoot. Do this for each of the targets and then look at the results. Because of the tight chokes, you can see exactly where the gun's point of impact is. Is it approximately the same on each target? If it's not, you are not being consistent with your mount. *(continued on page 24)*

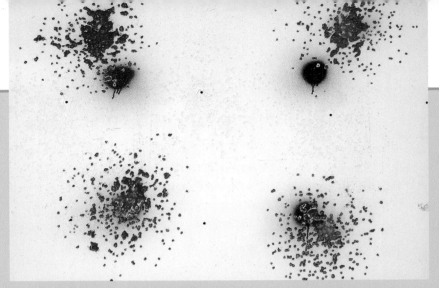

A pattern board example of an inconsistent mount. Note the shot strike high and left, high and right, dead on, and low and right.

(continued from page 23)

Before a gun can be correctly fitted to you, you must become consistent in your mount. If all the impacts are roughly the same (all equally high, low, left, or right) and not exactly on target, your mount is consistent but you have a gun fit problem.

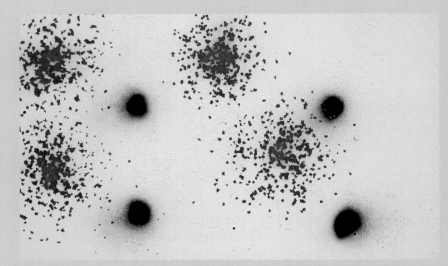

This is an example of a fairly consistent mount, but a poor stock fit. The shot strikes are consistently high and left, so the stock needs to be adjusted right and down by a large amount.

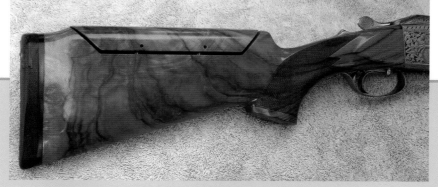

Above: *A Krieghoff adjustable comb. An adjustable comb allows for up and down adjustment and left-to-right adjustment so the eye is correctly positioned over the gun's rib.* **Below:** *A correctly fitted gun and consistent mount produces these results—four center-target shot strikes.*

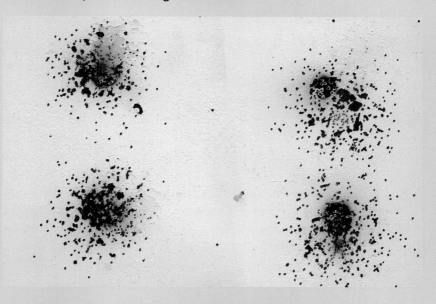

There are many solutions to gun fit problems. The simplest solution is an adjustable comb. If your gun does not have an adjustable stock or comb, the next best solution is to install an adjustable comb with both left/right adjustments (called cast) and up/down adjustments. Alternatively, you can tape one or more layers of moleskin or foam pads to the stock to increase stock height, or sand down the comb of the stock to lower stock height, or have a gunsmith bend the stock to achieve the correct left/right (cast) fit.

Until your gun shoots where you point it, your target-breaking success will be limited. If your impacts were consistent and all centered on the targets, your gun fits!

Shotgun Sights

Shotguns generally have at least a simple white bead at the end of the barrel rib. Target shotguns generally have a smaller steel mid-bead at the halfway point of the rib. The front and mid-bead should only be checked when pre-mounting the gun to ensure a proper gun mount. You should never look at the beads while you're shooting at a target. More about that in later chapters.

There is a wide variety of aftermarket shotgun beads. Most are larger than the factory beads, many are different colors, some even glow in the dark. Our advice is to stick with the smallest bead you can that has the

TOM'S TAKE I've shot a lot of different shotguns, and some are better than others. You get what you pay for. You can buy an over-and-under these days for less than $500. Or you can rob a bank with the $500 model and spend upward of $250,000 on a Holland & Holland. Either one will do the job, but one will last a whole lot longer than the other.

I started out hunting partridge with a 20-gauge Remington autoloader. It was a pretty good little gun with a short barrel, and I killed a lot of birds with it, but autoloaders can jam and need to be disassembled and cleaned frequently. I envied hunters with over-and-unders and, even more, the classic side-by-sides.

When I began to shoot clays, I bought a 12-gauge Remington 1100 autoloader, a very affordable gun, and learned to completely dismantle it so I could really clean it properly. I shot that gun a lot, and it is a formidable and dependable shotgun. Many championships have been won on the skeet field with a Remington autoloader. I installed a competition trigger and bought some aftermarket chokes, and I shot that gun for a long time.

Then one day I fell in love with a nifty little gun, a North American Versatile Hunting Dog Association (NAVHDA) gun. The gun is a 20-gauge Beretta Onyx with the forcing cones lengthened and the barrel cut down to 20 inches. No choke, just a cylinder bore. It's very easy to tote all day in the woods and kills birds out to 30 yards reliably. Because of the open barrel, it does not pepper the birds too hard.

The gun drew many curious onlookers. It looked like something you might use to rob a liquor store. But if ever there was a fun gun, this was it. I still use it in the woods during bird season. It is my all-time favorite field gun, but it is not really a clays gun.

most unobtrusive color—white. In other words, stay away from the after-market add-ons. They will only draw your eye away from the target, leading to a miss.

Barrel Length

Over the years, barrel lengths have become longer and longer. In general, longer is better if your build allows it.

The longer a barrel, the smoother it swings. But the additional length usually means more weight, especially on your forward hand. Additional weight out front can make the gun front heavy and difficult to swing

I purchased a Rizzini 12-gauge over-and-under, my first real clays gun, which came with all the chokes necessary to shoot my new favorite game. But the gun was heavy and awkward and the triggers were very heavy and creep-ridden.

I graduated to a Browning 625, and that was a very big step forward. Mark advised me that if I was going to dedicate myself to my new passion I should buy a quality gun that would last a lifetime. I decided to buy a Krieghoff K-80. A Krieghoff is a German shotgun built like a battleship. It is made to shoot hundreds of thousands of rounds and is the pinnacle of German engineering.

So I sold all my other guns and bought a $10,000 Krieghoff. (People who balk at the price should consider that many outdoorsmen buy motorcycles, skimobiles, camps, boats, and other expensive toys in that price range.)

And what a gun! It shoots like a dream, has triggers that break like glass, and balances like a scale.

Most other guns, with the possible exception of a Perazzi, are simply not built for the punishment of high-volume shooting. With a yearly service, a Krieghoff will last a lifetime.

Mark and I recommend buying your K-80 from Chris Maest of Clay Target Sports in Princeton, New Jersey. He will fit the gun to your personal specifications, and this makes all the difference in the world. Chris was a service manager for Krieghoff, so he knows his stuff.

Every expert recommends that you look around and try different guns. Choose the one that feels best to you, and make your own judgment. Most shooters are friendly folks and will let you try their gun if you ask nicely, which is a great way to experience new guns shooting at real targets.

instinctively. But if your arms are long and you can grip the front of the fore-end, a longer barrel won't feel front heavy.

For over-and-under guns, the popular favorite length for men right now is 32 inches. That's roughly equivalent to a 28-inch autoloader barrel. Women prefer 30-inch over-and-under barrels for their smaller builds. Large men with long arms can easily handle a 34-inch over-and-under barrel without sacrificing quickness.

If you prefer over-and-unders, the Krieghoff is the best buy in target guns. At $10,000, the standard model is more expensive than most other shotguns, but with over-and-unders, you get what you pay for.

Krieghoffs don't break or wear out ("shoot loose" in shotgun speak), and they are superbly balanced and have the best quality chokes and triggers on the market. They are the only target gun that you can shoot hard for five years and then sell for more than you paid for it.

Whether you buy a Beretta, Browning, Remington, Krieghoff, or some other gun, your sporting gun should be light enough to move instinctively and must fit correctly and possess the longest barrel you can comfortably swing.

Ammunition

There are a lot of different ammunitions for sporting clays: Fiocchi, Estate, White Rhino, Rio, Kamen, Nobel, Little Rhino, Winchester AA, Remington STS Premier, White Gold, Kent, Nitro Sporting Clays, and Winchester Super Sport. Whatever you buy, you need to know how it works in your gun with your chokes. In Maine we pattern our guns in the snow. It works beautifully. You can see the pattern size and pellet distribution perfectly.

The rules of sporting clays (and most clubs) limit shot weight and size to 1$1/8$ ounces of 7$1/2$ shot. With shotgun pellets, the larger the number, the smaller the shot size. There are three basic shot sizes commonly used for the clay target sports: 9 shot (the smallest and typically only used for skeet), 8 shot used in sporting clays and 16-yard trap, and 7$1/2$ shot—the heaviest and largest—used in handicap trap and sporting clays for long targets.

The larger the pellet, the heavier it is and the farther it will travel while retaining its energy. This translates into long-distance hits that break the target. Conversely, the smaller a pellet is, the lighter it is, which limits its travel and its striking power. But the tradeoff in pellet size is in the number of

Mark's New Shotgun

As I've aged and as the years of shooting heavy loads have caught up with me, I've recently shifted to the ultralight Beretta 391 autoloader. It is significantly lighter that a K-80, but it is superbly balanced. With a 30-inch barrel, it provides a very stable and smooth swing platform—perfect for long targets. I've shot Remington and Browning autoloaders, and while they are excellent guns, they don't come close to the Beretta 391 for reliability and point-ability. And the 391 has significantly less recoil, as does any autoloader shotgun compared to a solid-lockup gun like an over-and-under or pump gun. These are critical attributes for sporting clays, because a sporting clays shooter works his equipment hard.

Considering the cost of the Beretta 391 and its capabilities, it is a remarkable value and perfectly suited to our sport.

Some experts, like the great skeet shooter Wayne Mayes, have said it can take up to a year for a shooter to successfully adjust to a new gun. I did not have that problem but did have to adjust my hold points and style to make the new gun work well.

The 391 comes with an adjustable stock. It uses a shim system to allow for four height adjustments and two cast (right-left) adjustments. The factory settings are on the third height setting and a right-hand cast. So the first thing I did was check the gun's point of impact, figuring I would need to adjust the stock.

I tested the point of impact, and to my surprise, the stock was set perfectly for me. The 391 Urika 2 comes with a number of Optima bore chokes. These are very long extended-type chokes. (They extend from the muzzle so they can be changed without using a choke wrench—perfect for sporting clays.) All the Optima bore chokes are very tight. All the 391 Optima bore chokes marked modified or tighter qualify as full chokes when using 3-dram or 3 1/4-dram target loads. As long as you know this, it is not a problem.

Shooting the 391 has been a real pleasure. Even though the gun still feels long in my hands, it moves and points beautifully and hardly recoils at all. I can usually see the target break over the barrel because the gun does not buck or bounce up at all when it fires. It's like shooting a small-gauge gun.

This gun is a real bargain. It has proven to be very robust, requiring minimal cleaning. It is reliable, it points beautifully, and the typical price for a Urika 2 Sporting model 391 is about $1,250 as of this writing. That's one-tenth the price of a new standard-grade Krieghoff K80.

pellets in a given load. Because of the small size of 9 pellets, a 1¹/₈-ounce load contains 658 pellets, while a 7¹/₂ shot with 1¹/₈-ounce load will only hold 394 pellets. (See appendix C for more.)

The higher the pellet count in a given load, the better the pattern performance—less holes in the pattern and a better distribution of pellets within the pattern. Because of wind resistance, patterns using smaller shot sizes also tend to spread faster—in effect delivering a wider pattern for a given choke.

So how do we use this information to break targets in sporting clays?

First, we can discount 9 shot. Using typical chokes, it's only good for close shots—shots out to about 20 yards. A sporting course usually does not have enough shots this close to make carrying 9 shot ammo worthwhile.

Ammo with 8 shot is a good choice for most close to medium-distance targets up to 30 yards. Ammo with 8 shot has about 20 percent more striking power than 9 shot and retains its energy over a longer distance—it does not slow down as fast as 9 shot. This equates to a medium-distance target-breaking power that 9 shot does not have.

The king of target shot is 7¹/₂ shot. It retains its energy better than 8 or 9 shot, meaning it will travel farther at a faster speed than either of the other shot sizes. This equates to long-distance target-breaking power. As a rule, it patterns tighter than either of the other shot sizes. (Because the pellets are larger and heavier, they are not affected by wind resistance as much as the smaller shot sizes, resulting in tighter patterns for any given choke.)

To summarize, 9s usually aren't worth bothering with because they are limited to very close targets. Next, 8 shot ammo is perfect for close and medium distances to about 30 to 35 yards for almost all target presentations, and 7¹/₂ shot ammo is good for long-distance shots or hard-to-break targets like the rabbit target or medium-distance on-edge targets.

Ammunition velocity and charge weight are two other important considerations. Twelve-gauge target ammo generally comes in either 1-ounce or 1¹/₈-ounce shot charge. For any given velocity, the different charge weights will have considerably different recoils—the 1-ounce load will feel much lighter than the 1¹/₈-ounce load at the same velocity. A target shell's published velocity is expressed as either a foot-per-second value or as a DRAM equivalent value. The DRAM equivalent refers to the velocity produced by the smokeless powder equivalent weight of black powder. A typical 12-gauge target load is 3 DRAM equivalent 1¹/₈ ounce of 8 shot. In 1¹/₈-ounce load, the 3 DRAM equivalent powder charge corresponds to 1,200 feet-per-second—usually measured about 3 feet from the muzzle for U.S. manufactured ammo and at the muzzle for European manufactured ammo. With a 1-ounce load, the 3 DRAM equivalent is 1,250 feet-per-second (same powder charge, less payload equals more velocity). High velocity loads may advertise as MAX DRAM equivalent. This usually means 3 1/4 DRAM, or 1,250 feet-per-second for a 1 1/8-ounce load. The MAX term refers to the American Trap Association's maximum allowed velocity for ammo of 1,250 feet-per-second. This ammo may also be advertised as handicap or super handicap for velocity, indicating it is at or just below 1,250 feet-per-second.

The National Sporting Clays Association has no limit on a shell's velocity used in sporting clays. As a result, for very high velocities, ammo manufacturers actually advertise the velocity of their ammo in feet-per-second. Winchester has a 1,300 feet-per-second load called Super Sporting, Fiocchi has a 1-ounce Super Crusher at 1,350 feet-per-second, and Remington has a 1,300 feet-per-second load called Nitro Sporting. Both The high velocity Winchester and Remington shells are available in either 1- or 1 1/8-ounce loads.

There are few important points to keep in mind about high-velocity ammunition:

- They recoil much harder than the slower speed ammo. The gain in long-distance hitting power may come at a high cost if you're recoil sensitive.
- They slow down much faster than slower speed ammo. The 100-foot-per-second velocity increase 3 feet from the muzzle translates to only a 25-foot-per-second velocity increase at 50 yards.
- They cause the choke patterns to spread faster than slower ammo. This can be dramatic, so you must know how your ammo/choke combination works in your gun.

If you shoot an autoloader, we recommend a quality 3 DRAM, 1 1/8-ounce load of 8 shot for your all-purpose shell. This load will easily handle any target out to 35 yards (see the exceptions below). For targets beyond that distance, we recommend a 1,250-foot-per-second (MAX DRAM) load of 1 1/8-ounce 7 1/2 shot.

For solid-lockup shotguns like over-and-unders, side-by-sides or pump guns, we recommend 2 3/4 DRAM (1,150 foot-per-second) 1 1/8-ounce load of 8 shot for general-purpose use out to 30 to 35 yards, and

Remington Nitro 27s in 1 1/8-ounce 7 1/2 shot for anything over that distance. The Remington Nitro 27's perceived recoil is very light for their striking power.

There are a few exceptions to the above guidelines. Rabbit targets are very tough and hard to break. Use the heaviest shell you own for these targets regardless of the distance. Dying targets—targets that are at the very end of their flight and are slowly dropping to the ground—have almost no centrifugal energy because they are barely spinning. Targets in this state are harder to break that a fast-moving, fast-spinning target. We recommend that you use a heavy 7 1/2 shell for these targets no matter the distance.

Quality matters with ammunition. Each of the major U.S. manufacturers carry a line of premium ammo—Winchester AA and Remington STS Premier—and a line of economy target ammo—Remington Gun Club and Winchester Super X. The economy ammo uses softer lead, which leads to more shot deformation and wider patterns, and the faster burning powder results in more perceived recoil. With ammo, as with shotguns, you get what you pay for.

Perceived recoil refers to how your body feels a gun's recoil. All 3 DRAM, 1 1/8-ounce loads will generate identical total recoil in all guns. But based on the type of gun and the components in the shell, how each feels to you may be very different. An autoloader reduces felt recoil because its autoloading action spreads the total amount of recoil over a longer period of time using its main recoil spring. It will feel more like a push against the shoulder than a punch. A solid-lockup gun like an over-and-under or pump gun transmits all the recoil the instant it's generated as the shell fires. That will feel more like a punch in the shoulder. Slower burning gunpowders have the same effect. The slower the powder burns in the barrel at the instant of ignition, the less the perceived recoil because total recoil is spread out over a longer period of time.

Reloading

Shotgunners have been reloading their own shells since the days of black powder cartridges; it is an effective way to reduce the cost of shooting. Modern reloading machines are very reliable and reasonably priced, and a full range of reloading components (shot, wads, powder, and hulls) is readily available. Many trap and skeet shooters reload and achieve significant savings, but very few sporting clays shooters reload. One of the reasons is because sporting clays is primarily a 12-gauge game, and the only real sav-

ings in reloading is in the sub-gauges. There are sub-gauge events in sporting clays, but they are side events shot on softer courses and are generally
poorly attended. In skeet, the three sub-gauges are an integral part of the
game, so a competitive skeet shooter will shoot far more sub-gauge than
12-gauge and, therefore, realize significant savings by reloading. The other
reason not many sporting shooters reload is because reloads generally are
not allowed at tournaments. This is not an NSCA rule, but many large
clubs ban reloads for NSCA tournaments.

Chokes

Breaking a clay target with a shotgun using a target load is a game of odds.
You're not shooting a single projectile but a swarm of tiny pellets that act
randomly. To prove this, fire three or four times at a patterning board with
identical chokes, ammo, and gun. Each pattern will be completely different. They should be roughly the same size, but the pellet spread within
the strike area will be different with each shot. This effect gets more pronounced as the pattern opens up. Even choke experts can't explain why
chokes act the way they do, nor can they duplicate results with chokes.

Every shotgun pattern has a concentration of pellets at the center of the
pattern and a steadily decreasing density of pellets the farther away from
the center of the pattern you measure. This center density is called the core
of the pattern.

Choke and barrel performance experts believe that the closer a barrel
is to the standard .726-inch diameter 12-gauge bore size, the more dense—
or hotter—the core is. This is one reason barrel experts began over-boring (or back-boring) barrels. By opening up the bore diameter, fewer
pellets concentrated in the core of the pattern, resulting in a better distribution of pellets. Now many shotgun manufacturers over-bore their target shotgun barrels, sometimes to extreme amounts. This improves
open-choke performance with chokes like cylinder, skeet, and improved
cylinder. Depending on your gun's bore size, your most open chokes may
actually have a hot core and allow you to break targets much farther away
than conventional wisdom would suggest. This effect is especially preva-
lent with Italian guns, which generally don't over-bore their barrels, and
with older American guns made before over-boring was popular, like
Remington 1100 autos from the 1960s.

You can dramatically increase the odds of a kill if you use the correct
choke and ammo for a particular target presentation.

Imagine a 35-yard on-edge crossing target. You shoot at it with 1-ounce, 1,250 feet per second, $7^1/2$ shot ammo using cylinder (zero restriction) chokes in your gun. If you do everything right, you may break the target with this choke/ammo combination. Your chances of breaking it may even be as much as 75 percent, depending on how lucky you are that day and how hot the core of your pattern is. But a poor hit-to-miss ratio doesn't make for a good score.

Using my light-modified chokes (.015-inch restriction) and Federal paper $1^1/8$-ounce, 1,200 feet per second load of 8 shot, I can break this target ten out of ten times. Notice I said using *my* chokes and ammo. I've tested them, and I know how they perform. I don't know that about your chokes and ammo.

Note that the randomness of a choke pattern still applies, but by reducing the size of the pattern (from 6 feet to 30 inches) and increasing the number of pellets (from 350 to 461), we've vastly reduced the effects of the randomness. The pattern will still have holes, but with quality chokes and ammo those holes will be too small for a target to fly through.

Target types and presentations matter: the distance, how the target is presented, and what type it is. On edge, belly on, dome on, or some mix on a quartering target; rabbit, standard, midi or mini, and battue. Even tar-

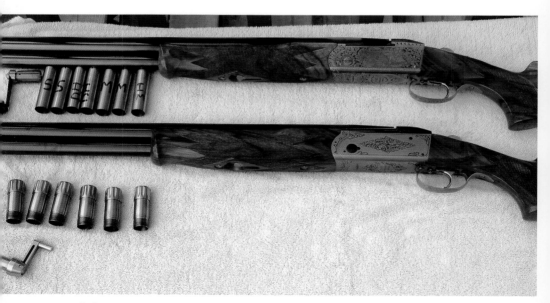

A shooter can never have too many guns or too many chokes.

Mark's Lesson on Heavy Shells

A number of years ago I found myself at a large regional tournament without any heavy ammo. I hadn't been using heavy shells at that time in Maine as most sporting courses were in heavily wooded areas with close targets. After dusting a number of 40-plus yard targets at this tournament, I decided to get something with some real punch. I bought a case of 1,300-feet-per-second, 1-ounce premium shells much favored by many FITASC shooters.

I used them for the second hundred of the tournament and did terribly with them. I missed many targets I felt sure would break. The following week, I hung a number of standard targets on posts 45 yards away. I wanted to test the ammo to see if something was wrong with the ammo or with me.

Using my light-mod chokes and the 1-ounce shells, I could not put one single pellet on a target, even after five tries shooting from bench rest. Almost any high-velocity 1-ounce load I tried with my light-modified choked would not break or even scratch one of those 45-yard hanging targets. But any 1 1/8-ounce load would break the target. If I tightened the chokes to modified (.020-inch restriction), the 1-ounce loads work perfectly.

I learned two lessons: One was that lead breaks targets, and more lead breaks more targets. The second was to know my equipment. I had no idea how those high-speed, 1-ounce shells would work in my gun. If I had known, I would have used much tighter chokes.

get speed matters. Faster targets break easier than slow targets because of wind resistance and spin energy. Crack a fast target with a 1-pellet hit, and the wind and its own centrifugal energy will likely tear it apart.

Appendix B contains an excellent sporting clays choke chart from Gil Ash at the OSP Shooting School. This chart gives detailed information on what chokes to use based on target type and distance.

There are a lot of variables to consider when selecting choke and ammo for a shot, but before you can determine what combination to use, you have to know how your chokes and ammo perform.

Instead of all the complex tests you've read about—like counting pellet holes in patterning paper—do a simple, real-world test of your ammo and choke combination: Break a target with it. Suspend a target from a post and then shoot at it from the farthest distance you would normally use that choke and ammo. You can hang the target so it presents itself as dome on, belly on, or whatever interests you. The results may surprise you. This is a realistic test of hitting power even though there is no centrifugal energy from spin or wind velocity to help break the target. It is becoming quite common to see very slow moving targets at the end of their flight path drifting to the ground with virtually no spin and at sometimes considerable distances. If your ammo and chokes can break a suspended target, they will break these drifting targets.

Because we've done target break testing of our equipment, we know light-modified chokes with a premium shell with 1¹/₈-ounce load of 8 shot will reliably break almost any dome-on standard target out to 45 yards. Light-modified did not work as well with edge-on targets at that distance.

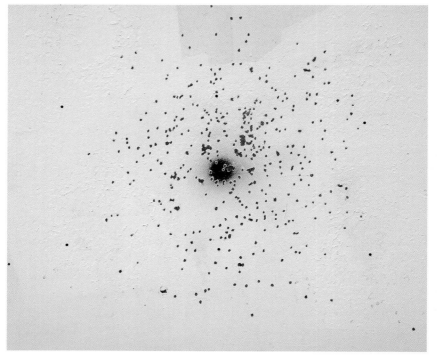

This is a classic blown pattern. With a skeet choke (.05-inch restriction) we would expect to see a 30-inch circle of pellet strikes at 20 yards. Here we have an almost 4-foot pattern. Quality chokes, quality ammo, unexpected results. The ammo used was 1,300-feet-per-second, 1¹/₈-ounce 7¹/₂ shot.

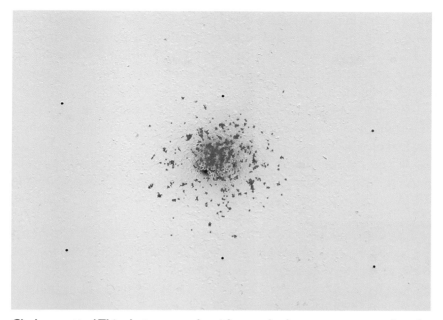

Chokes matter! This shot was made with exactly the same ammo and at the same distance as the previous pattern but with a Briley thin-walled, light-modified choke with .015-inch restriction.

But a modified choke using a quality handicap shell with 1^1/8 load of 7^1/2 shot did the trick.

Another component of choke and ammo selection is the ability to judge distances. It does no good to know just what your chokes do at a measured 40 yards if you can't tell how far away a target is when it's in flight.

Here's a simple way to learn to judge distances: Use a measuring device like a laser range finder to measure the distance to all the significant landscape features and trap locations from the typical shooting stations at your favorite club. When you shoot this measured course or station, think about the distance of the targets you're shooting in relation to the objects you've measured. Over time, you'll become quite familiar with what targets look like at various distances.

Ammo has many variables. Sure, a handicap or heavy sporting 1^1/8-ounce premium target load of 7^1/2 shot will break any target we're ever likely to see on a sporting course, close or far. But who wants to take a pounding like that if you don't have to? Autoloaders reduce felt recoil to some extent, but heavy loads will still pound you. And the effects of recoil on the body are cumulative. Also, heavy recoil will require you to hold on tighter to the gun, possibly reducing the fluid movement that is so important to a smooth swing and making it more difficult to make a good move to the second target.

When it comes to choke and ammo selection, there is no such thing as too much information. If you don't know how your equipment performs, you're firing blind.

As you test your ammo and chokes, you will likely determine an all-purpose choke for your gun and ammo combination. This choke should

TOM'S TAKE   When do I change chokes? What choke do I use for which targets? How many chokes should I own?

I am the slowest choke changer on the planet. I often feel rushed when it comes time to change chokes, especially if I am the first up to shoot. It's distracting. I would rather look at the show birds than the muzzle of my shotgun. I feel more serene if I can devote all my attention to the targets. I would rather immerse myself in the details of the target presentation than fool around with my chokes. But choke and ammo matter. I've seen dramatic evidence of that on long shots.

I own two skeet chokes, one improved-cylinder, two light-modified, one modified, one improved-modified, and one full choke. I know some shooters—good friend and ace shot Buzz Mendoza, for one—who shoot nothing but modified and modified.

Another good friend and master gunsmith, Chris Maest of Clay Target Sports, suggests that improved cylinder and light modified should work very well on most sporting clay courses. I've heard that the great British shots favor full and full, but I think that's overdoing it. I often shoot light modified and light modified, and that's it. I can pay strict attention to the birds and forget about changing chokes altogether. But is this really wise?

I went out and bought a full choke just to try it. Boy, does a full choke pulverize targets! But it is unforgiving on close targets. However, on very long targets I found it gives an added measure of confidence.

I use cylinder bore for the closest of close targets, knowing that cylinder bore means no choke at all. I use skeet for skeet and improved cylinder for a good all-around choke out to 30 yards or so. Light modified is another good all-be able to break any target up to about 40 yards without penalizing you too much on medium-close targets of around 20 yards. An all-purpose choke should work well from 20 to 40 yards. Beyond 40 yards, use either a modified or improved modified choke. Closer than 20 yards, use either a cylinder or skeet choke. In a Krieghoff, using the ammo we use, the all-purpose sporting choke is light modified. For the Beretta 391, it is the Optima bore improved cylinder choke.

You don't need to change chokes for every target, but be prepared to if necessary. Evaluate every target during preview to make sure the standard choke—for your gun/ammo combination—will do the job. If the

around choke that can also handle some distance. This knowledge comes from a lot of time at the patterning board with Mark.

Modified is the beginning of a very tight choke setup followed by improved modified, almost full in effect, and then full itself.

Experimentation is key in determining what works best for your gun. As with handguns and rifles, some ammos are more accurate than others. I have also discovered that different chokes work differently, and that one man's light modified is another man's improved cylinder.

I have been shooting light mod and light mod almost exclusively with the exception of really close targets. I prefer not to screw around with my chokes and instead devote my full attention to the birds. But I wonder if by sticking to the same chokes I am hurting myself.

Get your gun and chokes out, buy some different ammo in different strengths and sizes, set up a patterning board, and have some fun! You will learn a lot about your ammo and your chokes that will prove helpful at the club. Mark and I spent a lot of time patterning my gun and its different chokes and trying out different ammos. It is time-consuming but well worth the effort.

I also urge you to reach into your wallet and buy some quality choke tubes. Pure Gold and Briley both make some excellent chokes. Most chokes today can be screwed in by hand and are much quicker to change than in years past, when you had to use a wrench.

Most of us have had the good fortune to break a target at a seemingly impossible distance. The goal is to put the lead in the right place so the target breaks almost all the time. Chokes can help with this but are not a cure-all for missing targets.

target is an unusual presentation or extremely close or far, change chokes and ammo as necessary.

It's all about stacking the odds in your favor.

Safety

A shotgun can be a particularly devastating firearm. A gun accident can have tragic consequences. There is simply no room for error with a shotgun. You must always respect its lethal power.

Some simple rules always apply:

- Don't ever point a gun at anyone for any reason.
- Always assume the gun is loaded. That will ensure that you respect its deadly potential.
- Break the gun open or open the action whenever you are not on a shooting station.
- Never load the gun unless you are on the shooting station. Keep the barrel pointing downrange and never load more than two shells (sometimes three for specific events).
- Always wear eye and ear protection.
- Don't be shy when it comes to correcting the unsafe gun-handling habits of others. Speak up! You may save a life.

If you are in the company of new shooters, talk to them about gun safety. No one wants to get hurt because he or she failed to follow common-sense safety precautions.

If you shoot with a hunting gun, or one with a manual safety, you may need to take off the safety every time you shoot. Pay close attention and make sure you know whether the safety is on or off.

Many competitive shooters lock their safety in the off position so that they are not distracted by a safety that can slip or be nudged into the safe position. Locking or otherwise deactivating the safety may seem like a safety issue itself, but consider that many aftermarket competition triggers for autoloaders do not even have a safety, and most high-grade competition over-and-under shotguns have some built-in mechanism for locking their safety in the off position. Locking safeties off makes sense because—when shooting at an organized club—the gun is never loaded until the shooter is on a shooting station and the gun is pointing downrange. This is the no. 1 rule of gun safety at any shooting club. At many clubs, failure to follow this basic rule can get you immediately expelled from the club.

Even when in a gun rack, autoloaders and pump guns must have their actions open.

Pump and autoloaders must have their bolts open, and breech-break guns like side-by-sides and over-and-unders must be broken open and stay that way at all times. Gun clubs have amazingly good safety records, and this basic rule is the biggest reason why.

Eye protection is mandatory at most shooting clubs and is required at all NSCA tournaments. Pellets can ricochet off a target, and pieces from broken targets can fall on participants. (See page 52 for more about eye protection.)

It seems obvious, but do not shoot if you have been drinking or taking prescription medication that may affect your judgment or abilities. It's not worth the risk. Maine—like most states—has a zero-tolerance law for drinking in the field, and the same regard for safety applies while shooting clays. Be safe and you will never be sorry.

And finally, a word about reloads: if you plan on reloading your own shells, get expert advice on how to do it. Too much powder, or a poorly constructed shell, can yield disastrous results.

A new shooter at the club once was having trouble operating his brand new autoloader. There was nothing wrong with it; he just didn't know how to operate it. And there were shells in the gun. If you don't know how your gun works, find someone who does and learn how to operate it.

No matter what gun you own, take the time to get to know your gun and how it works before you go shooting. Safety is no accident!

Seeing the Target

In the U.S. Navy, the computer that points the big guns at targets is called the fire control computer. It receives distance, speed, direction, and range-to-target information from the gun's radar, and then it calculates the gun's traverse and elevation, taking into account the ship's roll, speed, and direction. It is amazingly accurate.

You also have a fire control computer—in your brain. With plenty of programming (practice) and given the right input (from your eyes), your fire control computer can direct your shotgun to hit a 60+ mph target many yards away. And a standard dome target seen on edge presents only about a 4-square-inch surface area to shoot at. When it's dome-on, it's still only about 14 square inches.

Your brain is quite a computer, but it cannot work unless it gets good input. It's not enough to see a vague shape moving in front of a tree line. In order for your brain to automatically calculate gun speed and leads, your eyes—both eyes—must clearly see the target and have a hard focus on it. Your brain cannot determine the distance to an object unless both eyes are focused on the object.

Hard focus means to concentrate so hard on seeing the target that you are oblivious to visual distractions. A bird flying by in your peripheral vision is invisible; you never see it. An empty target box gets blown into your kill zone and you never notice. But you can see the rings on the spinning target. That's hard focus. You concentrate all your energy on seeing the target, and you practice it over and over again.

TOM'S TAKE

They say you can't stare at the target hard enough. What precisely does this mean? Doesn't seeing it fly through the air make you look at it hard enough? And what about targets that are hard to see, like a dark target against a dark background or a bird that is on edge or a target that is flying through a very narrow window? Some birds just seem to be extra hard to acquire, particularly the fast ones. All sporting clays shooters have had the

A shot of the woods at Hermon Skeet Club. Can you see the target?

In sporting clays, you will always have an opportunity to preview a target, either as the lead-off shooter in the cage or by viewing the targets behind a shooter. During the preview, mark where you first see the target, even as just a flash of orange. This is the target pickup point. Mark where you obtain a solid focus on it—the focus point. Note its trajectory and speed. During the preview, you'll begin to get a feel for the target. Note

experience of a bird being launched and never seeing it at all! "Where did that go?" we will cry.

When the bird first flies, all you see is a blur. When does it slow down enough for you to lock onto it without it being too far gone?

One thing is clear—you can't hit what you can't see!

Another great woods shot at Hermon. The target is a little easier to see this time!

Target preview is the time to locate the visual pickup point, the hold point, and the target break point.

where the target travels to. Look for the perfect spot to break the target and your gun hold point, where you will position the gun when you call for the target. When you are done previewing targets, you should be able to draw an imaginary line through the sky that exactly duplicates the target's travel.

A basic principle of wing shooting is that the longer you see a target in flight, the better your brain can process the incoming data from your eyes. When you're ready to call for the target, your eyes should be looking at the target pickup point—that is, where the target first becomes visible, even as just a flash of orange. You should never be looking over the gun barrel for the target unless the target is flying straight away from you. Where you position the gun when you call for the targets—your hold point—is based on the type of swing you're going to use to break the target, whether it's swing-through, sustained lead, or pull-away. (See chapter five for more on these swing styles.)

The gap between the target's visual pickup point and your gun hold point represents time—time for your fire control computer to evaluate the target, time to bring the shotgun up to the target's speed, and time to mount the gun.

The Barrel

You should always know where your muzzle is; you should see it in your peripheral vision as a shape below your direct line of sight. When your gun is at its hold point, the muzzle should be just below the target's flight path. No matter how you move the gun, you maintain focus only on the target as it flies. But by using your peripheral vision, you remain aware of and control your barrel's position. It's like driving your car. As you drive, you look only at the road in front of you, but you see your car's hood in your peripheral vision.

This leads into another important point about seeing the target. Trap and skeet shooters fully mount the gun before they call for the target. Even though this severely obstructs vision, it works well for them. They always know where every target is coming from and going to and they practice the gun swing required to break the same trap and skeet target thousands and thousands of times. Some advanced skeet shooters never obtain a hard focus on the target. They can quite effectively shoot the target when they only see the initial flash of orange. This works because the targets are repetitive. They are not using their shooting brain to break targets so much as ingrained muscle memory.

Stare at the target, but control your barrel from your peripheral vision.

A sporting clays shooter must completely see the target in order to fully engage his shooting brain. Muscle memory won't work because of the infinite variety of target presentations. You should only rarely use a full gun mount prior to calling for the target in sporting clays, generally on trap-type targets where the target flies straight away from you. Restricting the view of the target means restricting the data input to your fire control computer.

When preparing to shoot the target, you should use either a true low-gun position—where the butt stock is below the armpit—or a semi-mounted gun, unless the target is in front of you and rising, as a trap target does. In these cases a fully mounted gun does not restrict your vision, and this type of target generally requires a very quick shot.

In the semi-mounted position, your butt stock is in or near your shoulder pocket, but your head is slightly raised off the gun stock and the muzzle is at its hold point slightly below the target's line. This gun position is quickly gaining in popularity because it eliminates the potential mounting problems of true low gun (the dreaded bobble), but it does not restrict target view at all. It allows for full peripheral vision, which is important in establishing the gap—the distance between where you first see the target and your gun's hold point.

George demonstrates the classic low-gun stance. Note how he keeps the barrel up on the target's line.

Another good reason for not using a fully mounted gun more than you have to when calling for the target is the longer the gun is intruding into your vision, as it does when the gun is fully mounted, the more likely your eyes are to focus on the rib or bead instead of on the target. The flight characteristics of the object that your eyes focus on feeds data to your shooting brain. This information allows you to move the gun at the necessary speed and subconsciously calculate the required lead. By shifting focus from the target to the bead or rib before or during the gun swing, the data stream to the brain that is so necessary to synchronizing with and breaking the target is completely disrupted. Imagine this: A feedback loop exists between your eyes, brain, and hands. Your eyes see the target move and tell your brain, which instructs your hands to move the gun. Your eyes see the gun move in your peripheral vision and tell your brain, which tells

An example of a semi-mounted gun. Head up and away from the butt stock; barrel on the target's line. You have full peripheral vision, but no bobble as you fully mount the gun.

What* not *to focus on.

your hands what to do to synchronize the barrel to the target, and so on. This occurs at a level far below conscious thought and continues from visual pickup, to swing, to mount, to shoot. But the feedback loop is broken if your eyes are not focused on the target. If the barrel intrudes too long into your vision, it will draw the eyes' focus away from the target.

The immediate result of looking at the barrel is that your gun slows down, leading to a miss behind. The solution is to keep your head off the gun for as long as possible until you're ready to make the shot.

Eye Dominance

Eye dominance is an intriguing phenomenon that directly affects how we shoot at moving targets. Even though we have two eyes, only one eye looks directly at the target. The other eye sees the target, but at an offset angle. That angle of offset is what gives us depth perception—the ability to judge distances. In this respect our eyes work exactly like an optical range finder. The problem arises when we have a dominant eye that does not match our dominant hand, called cross dominance. A right-handed person with cross dominance mounts the shotgun on his right shoulder, but his left eye looks

Shooting Glasses

Your choice of shooting glasses will also determine how well you see the target. Common sense, shooting clubs, and the NSCA all mandate wearing eye protection while shooting. Because sporting clays is shot in open fields and heavy forest, with targets flying directly into the sun, or in any combination of conditions on the same course, the sport demands a lot from shooting glasses. In order to see the targets under all these lighting conditions, your glasses must work for you.

New shooters often believe that off-the-shelf sunglasses or their everyday glasses will work well enough, but they will cost you targets.

Shooting glasses are designed for the head-forward stance used by shotgunners. They generally have no rims around the lenses because those rims will obstruct peripheral vision, which is especially critical for sporting clays because targets are never in the same place from station to station on a typical course.

Shooting glasses generally sit higher on your face to accommodate the head-forward position, and if they have prescription lenses, the ocular center of the lens is higher than on normal glasses for the same reason. One popular manufacturer even named their line of shooting glasses after the facial fit unique to shooters—the Decot High-Wyde glasses.

The lens tint you use—if any—is also very important. An American skeet many-time world champion once recommended using only as dark a lens as needed to eliminate squinting and no more. This becomes especially important as you age. The older a shooter gets, the more light he needs to see well because of the normal aging and dimming of the lens in the eyes.

Selecting what lens to use under varying conditions is a lot like making your choke selections. You may own many different lens colors, but over time you will more than likely settle on one all-purpose lens for bright conditions and one for low-light conditions. We've settled on a light purple lens that attenuates 15 percent light for bright conditions and a light yellow lens for dim conditions. Some shooters use a red lens and some prefer a gold or bronze lens, all of which have a red component to enhance the appearance of an orange target. There is no formula for which lens color to use in any given condition—your choice of lens color depends on how your eyes work and how old you are.

In trap and skeet, a shooter will select his lens tint at the beginning of an event and use the same lens for the entire event, rarely if ever changing lenses

Note how high Dave's glasses sit on his face. High mount, no rims: perfect shooting glasses.

while shooting. But that doesn't work well for sporting clays because of the many different lighting conditions you encounter during a single event. If you have separate frames for each lens tint, you can quickly change tints while shooting.

Keep in mind that what works for someone else won't necessarily work for you. A lens color that is marketed as the latest and greatest innovation to shooting rarely is. Colors can enhance a target's visibility, but ultimately any tint in a lens will reduce the light reaching your eyes. So a tint that enhances visibility under one circumstance may cause you problems under a different circumstance. Trial and error is the only way to determine what works best for you.

Some popular lens colors. Most tints have a red component to enhance the orange of the target, and light yellow is universally accepted as the best tint for low-light conditions.

directly at the target. His right eye—the eye aligned over the barrel's rib—sees the target but at an offset angle. Eye dominance develops in males during adolescence, and an estimated 30 percent of adult males are either cross dominant or have no dominant eye. Most women have no dominant eye.

Here is a quick self-test to determine your eye dominance. Start by standing square to a small object at least 10 feet away. Point the index finger of your non-dominant hand—the one that holds the fore-end and points the gun—at this object. Make sure you keep both eyes open and fully extend your arm when pointing. Holding this position, close your right eye. If your finger is pointing directly at the object, you are left-eye dominant. If the finger is no longer pointing at the object, open your right eye and close your left eye. If your finger is now pointing directly at the object with only the right eye open, you are right-eye dominant. If your finger does not point directly at the object with either your right eye only or left eye only open, you have no dominant eye—you have central vision.

If your dominant eye does not match your dominant hand, you are cross dominant. If you have central vision—no dominant eye—the problems you will experience when shooting are essentially the same as if you were cross dominant. Additionally, even though you may test with normal eye dominance, your eyes can shift dominance due to fatigue, stress, age, and even because of certain target types. A low comb can cause a dominance shift by partially blocking the dominant eye, causing the non-dominant eye to look directly at the target.

The bottom line is this: The eye aligned over the rib must be looking directly at the target at all times. Any other condition than this will lead to missed targets.

Cross dominance (and no dominance) is much more problematic for shotgunners than for rifle or pistol shooters, and within the clay target community it poses a more severe problem for sporting clays shooters than for either trap or skeet. With a shotgun mounted, the eye on the side of your face touching the comb of the butt stock should be the rear sight. That's what gun fit is all about—aligning your pupil directly over the rib when the gun is mounted. If you're right-handed but left-eye dominant, your left eye acts as the rear sight but is a few inches out of position.

Imagine shooting a rifle with the rear sight moved 3 inches to the left. You're not going to hit much—the same thing happens with a shotgun.

TOM'S TAKE My left eye is dominant, but I shoot right-handed. If I were a kid, I would try to learn to shoot left-handed so my shotgun mount would match my dominant eye.

When I look down my right-side mounted shotgun, my left eye wants to take over—it looks as if there are two barrels and one of them is sticking way out to the right. It wasn't until I took a simple eye-dominance test that I discovered the problem.

I have tried to shoot with both eyes open, as many great shooters recommend, but it doesn't work at all for me.

I tried a patch on my left eye, a small bit of Scotch tape over the left lens of my shooting glasses, but that caused problems catching left-to-right targets.

So I shoot with my left eye closed. I try to acquire the target with both eyes and close my left eye as I shoot, but I don't always succeed. For better or worse I am a one-eyed shooter. There aren't many like me out there, but there are a few good ones.

What should I do? Should I continue to shoot one-eyed or try something new?

Off-eye dominance or no-eye dominance also creates the multiple images Tom describes above, causing all sorts of visual confusion for the shooter.

Your eyes are the data input mechanism for your shooting brain. If you're seeing multiple barrels or multiple targets, your fire control computer gets totally confused. With trap and skeet, because of the repetitive nature of the targets and no need to judge distances, shooting one-eyed is not a major handicap. But in sporting clays, because of the infinite variety of targets, anything that reduces visual acuity is going to cause problems.

The best solution to eye-dominance issues is to shift the gun mount to the opposite shoulder, but for most older people that's very difficult or impossible to do. If you have an eye-dominance problem, try that first, though. You can also try to shoot with both eyes open for a few weeks at known-distance targets such as trap or skeet targets. Some shooters have reported that the ghosted barrel disappears after a few weeks of shooting, as the brain eventually blanks it out.

If you don't have success with shifting shoulders or shooting with both eyes open, try using a patch or blinking the dominant eye as you shoot. The patch works for many people and cures the double-vision issue, but it has a cost. Using the patch restricts peripheral vision on the side it's used on. The same is true with blinking the dominant eye as you shoot. What really happens is you close your eye when you mount the gun because that's when the double vision occurs. This totally eliminates peripheral vision on the non-dominant side. You should try blinking only as a last resort because it restricts vision more than the patch.

Certain targets may cause your non-dominant eye to assume dominance, leading to misses. In our experience these target types are close, very slow-moving targets or targets going almost straight away from you. If you experience inexplicable misses on a certain type of target, you may be experiencing a transient eye-dominance shift. Try closing your off-side eye as you mount the gun.

If you have tested as cross dominant and you've decided to use the patch, you'll need a half-inch circle of Scotch tape or equivalent material and a helper to install it. Correct position of the patch is essential. Here's how to install it: With the gun fully mounted, your head on the comb, and your eye perfectly aligned over the rib, close the non-dominant eye (the one over the rib). Have your helper position the patch on the off-side lens so that the patch is centered on the shotgun's front bead. This will effectively block the off-side (dominant) eye from seeing the barrel and target with the gun fully mounted.

One of the core shooting principles we'll discuss at some length in later chapters is the idea of limiting how long you ride a target with the gun fully mounted. Less is generally better. The later in the shot that you fully mount the gun, the more time your fire control computer has to evaluate the target. If you use the eye blink or patch method to solve an eye-dominance problem, it's even more important to come to the gun late in the shot because when you do fully mount the gun your vision is cut in half.

Eye dominance problems are handicaps you have to compensate for, but you can overcome them and still shoot very well.

CHAPTER 4

Set Up to Shoot

Stance

The body positioning in preparation for the shot is called stance, and foot position is a primary component. If your feet are out of position, it's very difficult to get the gun in the right place and moving in the correct manner to break the target. You will run out of swing room, slow the gun down, be out of balance, and probably sling the gun wildly and miss the target.

If your feet are properly positioned, you will be in a comfortable position to make the shot without your body binding up and slowing the gun swing; you'll be smoother, on line with the target, and much more likely to break it.

Try to think like a boxer: You have to be light on your feet and oriented correctly to the target. If you shoot without correct orientation to the target, you are handicapping yourself.

Without the correct foot position for the shot, nothing else really matters. Leads—or forward allowances—don't work, the best swing in the world doesn't work, and burning incense to the gods of sporting clays doesn't work. Shooting at a moving target with a shotgun is a whole body exercise. Your entire body must be involved, starting with your feet.

Your stance is the position you are in when you call for the targets: your body posture, angle to target, and the weight distribution on your feet. Your stance is not static but will change based on the target trajectory and speed.

Note George's foot position. With the gun pointing straight ahead at 12 o'clock, his front foot points to 1 o'clock and his back foot points to 3 o'clock. Set up this way, he can swing about 75 degrees left and 75 degrees right, pivoting on his front knee without rolling his shoulders or losing his balance.

I first started shooting moving targets when I took up bird hunting. Before that I was a bull's-eye shooter; I shot stationary targets with a rifle and a pistol. I wanted to get better at wing shooting, so I joined a clay targets club. But the form needed to succeed in sporting clays was completely foreign to me. A bird flew; you raised the gun and fired. Simple. That's all I knew, like a lot of bird hunters. But I missed more birds than I cared to, and I continue to see this lack of form all the time. A boxer needs to focus on his fighting stance, and a sporting clays shooter needs to focus on form.

If you can, watch a good sporting clays shot. You'll see a smooth mount, a gentle swing, and a dead bird, time after time, just like a machine. Smoothness, consistency, economy of motion—those are functions of good fundamentals. The basics of stance, addressing the target, and gun handling are the focus of this book. There are some great shooting coaches in sporting clays who have written many good books and made DVDs, but few spend enough time on the basic skills needed to achieve good form.

When I started shooting clays I relied on my old field methods—raise up and shoot. It's just not enough. You have to learn how to swing your gun as smoothly as a tennis player does his racket or a golfer his club. Form is function!

I see all manner of mounts at the range: muzzles pointed straight down, muzzles pointed straight up in the air, even muzzles turned sideways. I used a low gun position, and while I thought I was terribly sporting, I was making a severe tactical error. Mark looked at my feet as I set up to shoot and shook his head in wonder.

When I started out I didn't think very much about the position of my feet, and it wasn't until I began to think about my feet on every bird that I began to get better. How you stand and move when you shoot is so critical to being a good shotgunner that it amazes me how little attention is paid to it.

What should I do with my body, and by this I mean my entire body, to make sure I shoot well?

Let's break down a shooter's stance for a typical medium–high crossing target that you want to break at about 12 o'clock on a clock face.

Your lead foot (left foot for right-handed shooters) should be pointing toward 1 o'clock and your right foot toward 3 o'clock. Your feet should be

Front knee slightly bent, leaning forward from the ankles.

about shoulder-width apart and positioned so that a line drawn from your right heel passing through your left toes points directly at the break point—in this case, 12 o'clock. (Reverse this for left-handed shooters.)

Positioning yourself using the imaginary line seems cumbersome at first, but with repetition it will soon become automatic. Now lean forward from your ankles (not your waist), slightly bending your forward knee until about 60 to 70 percent of your weight is on your forward foot. This

George uses just enough pressure on the fore-end to control the gun and no more.

Note how George's knuckles are turning white because he is gripping the fore-end too much. This will cause a loss of fine motor control in his left hand, making it difficult to swing the gun smoothly.

is the classic nose-over-toes posture the big dogs use. It's important not to exaggerate this stance.

Too much forward lean or too much bend in the knees creates unnecessary muscle tension. This must be a relaxed and comfortable position for you.

The gun should rest in your hands without any significant muscle tension anywhere—pay special attention to your hands, arms, and shoulders. Apply just enough pressure to control the gun.

Left: George sets up for a target break point slightly above the horizon. Right: George sets up for a high target break point. Note that most of his weight is on his back foot. This weight distribution allows him to keep his head on the gun, even when pointing the gun straight up.

Left: *An aggressive stance prepares you for a low or very fast target.* **Right:** *This is a poor stance—too much weight is on the rear foot and his head is too far back on the stock as a result.*

One of the early great shooting instructors in the United States, D. Lee Braun, said you should "grip the fore-end like it was made of eggs."

Too much muscle tension anywhere in your body will reduce your ability to swing the gun effectively. When you squeeze the gun too tightly or tighten up your shoulder or arm muscles, you lose fine motor control. As we'll see in later chapters, when you're focused on the target and swinging the gun, hundreds of commands are being sent from your brain to your hands, arms, shoulders, and lower body to allow you to make all the subtle moves required to stay synchronized with the target. If your

TOM'S TAKE All this work on form has really paid off for me. For one thing, I no longer run out of room, like a spring that has been twisted too dramatically. Smooth swings have helped me tremendously on droppers and rabbits. My feet are in a much better position, and this helps me shoot a more controlled shot and eliminates a wild swing of the shotgun barrel. I have learned that if you do not pay attention to proper setup, you pay a high price in lost birds. Many a time I have missed a bird only to have Mark make a correction in my setup; then I smash the target.

This is one area where you can really improve your game without too much effort. When you get on the shooting pad, take that extra time to analyze your stance and make sure you are properly set up.

muscles have too much tension, they will not respond to the commands your brain sends, making it difficult or impossible to move smoothly with the target.

To illustrate this point, perform the following simple test. Write your name out in longhand as you normally would. Now tighten up your hand, wrist and arm muscles and write your name out in longhand again at the same speed as the first time. The difference is dramatic, and it feels jerky and uncomfortable. Now imagine swinging the gun and trying to make hundreds of subtle moves with that same jerky feeling and loss of control.

Relaxed muscles are the key to smooth, fluid movement. With your gun up and at your hold point, you're ready to call for the target.

Remember, weight distribution for a medium-high target should be roughly 60-40 on your front foot. If the target's trajectory is higher, your stance should shift more weight to the back foot until you have virtually all your weight on your back foot with the gun pointing nearly straight up. The opposite is true if the target trajectory is lower. The lower the target at the break point, the more weight should be on the forward foot.

Imagine a platform shooting station on a cliff or over a steep ravine (a setup used at the U.S. Open in '07). The target trajectory is under your feet, so you're pointing almost straight down at the break point. For this stance, all your weight should be on your forward foot.

Another example of poor stance: There is far too much knee bend, which increases overall lower body muscle tension to the point that any pivot at the ankles and knees is going to be awkward and jerky.

The reason behind the weight distribution is to allow you to pivot on your forward knee for all target heights and to keep your head on the gun stock while you're pivoting.

Target speed may also affect your stance. If a target requires a quick move, preloading your leg and arm/hand muscles will reduce your reac-

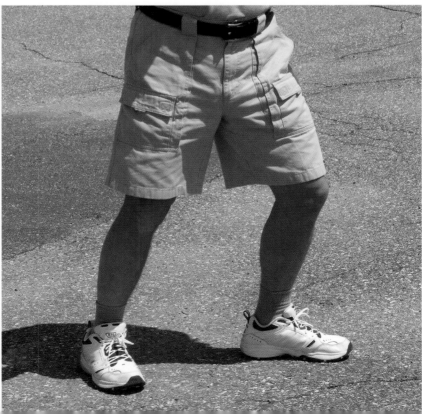

Facing page, top: *The key to smooth movement is in the knees and ankles. In this picture George begins to swing on a left-to-right crosser.* **Facing page, bottom:** *Halfway through the swing, he has flexed his knee as he turned his waist to the right.* **Above:** *The swing is complete, and his upper body has pivoted about 90 degrees by twisting at the ankles and flexing his forward knee.*

tion time, making you quicker to the target. To preload your leg muscles, crouch slightly and shift more weight to your forward foot. The same idea applies to your gun. Increase your grip pressure slightly. We will refer to this posture in later chapters as an aggressive stance. Be careful, though, that you don't go overboard preloading your muscles. You will quickly lose control of your swing if you do.

As we'll see later, the key to sporting clays is the swing. Correct stance is the foundation on which a great swing is built.

CHAPTER 5

Gun Swing and Speed

If you have ever gone fly fishing, you know how important it is to have a smooth swing. Without a smooth move in casting a fly, the line will get tangled and the fly will never go where you want it to.

In so many sports, swinging an implement is crucial to success. Baseball has a bat, hockey has a stick, golf has a club, tennis has a racket. In each of these games how well the player controls his implement and uses it effectively determines his or her success, and the same is true in sporting clays.

Good shooters swing not only very smoothly but with a terrific economy of motion. Here's why: Let's assume your gun shoots exactly where you point it when your pupil is correctly positioned over the rib. Now raise your head just an eighth of an inch from the stock. If you tested the point of impact now at 20 yards, you'd see that the center of your pattern moved up about 10 inches. No big deal at 20 yards because with skeet chokes in your gun you have a 30-inch pattern at 20 yards.

But double the distance to the target to 40 yards, and now that pupil raised an eighth of an inch causes your point of impact to be 20 inches

George arm-swings the gun because his feet aren't set correctly, binding his body's swing. Note how he pulls the gun off his face, effectively moving the rear sight, his right eye, far to the left.

TOM'S TAKE   I all too often roll my shoulders on a long crosser or muscle the gun in an effort to get on the bird, forcing a shot that should be graceful and easy. Also, because of poor hold points, I often bobble the muzzle of the gun as I swing, trying to get onto the bird. Or I hold too tightly onto the gun, losing fine motor control. How does a good swing improve my game and why is it so important? How does a good hold point smooth out the swing?

high. You likely missed the target. Now imagine that gun bobbles a little as you fire it. Just a quarter inch of muzzle bobble will be 40 inches off at 40 yards—a clean miss.

The point is that the smallest irregular movement in the gun has a more pronounced effect on your point of impact the farther away the target is. Any misalignment of your body with the gun will have the same effect.

If you arm-swing the gun because your feet are out of position and you can't swing correctly, you'll push the gun away from your face, moving the rear sight to the left if you are a right-handed shooter. You'll miss in front or behind depending on the direction of the target.

If you haven't flexed your left knee and you're standing flatfooted, your right shoulder will roll down as you swing on a left-to-right crosser. That shoulder roll pulls the gun off the target's line. If you pull it off-line just an eighth of an inch, you'll miss by 20 inches at 40 yards. You can see why a smooth swing is so important.

Swing Basics

There are a number of different types of swings used on different target types, but all swing types have much in common. First, you swing the gun with your whole body. The swing begins from the position we discussed earlier. For a typical crosser, your forward knee is flexed, weight is about 60-40 on the front foot, leaning slightly forward with feet aligned for your intended break point, gun at your hold point and eyes looking at the target pickup point.

When you first see the target, you begin to move the gun along the target's path, guiding it with your forward hand. You swing the body from

George rolls his right shoulder down because he's trying to swing flat-footed. This pulls the gun off-line, causing a miss.

your ankles up, pivoting at the ankles and flexing on your forward knee with your forward hand, steering the gun. Your forward hand leads, and your body follows. Your whole body should pivot, not just your shoulders or arms. By pivoting your entire body, you won't bobble the gun, roll your shoulders, or push the gun away from your face to catch the target. The ankle and knee pivot to keep everything aligned while you swing the gun and make controlling the gun during the swing much easier.

Whether you use true low-gun or a semi-mounted ready position, you swing the gun on the target's line before you mount (or come to) the gun. So in the progression of the swing, you see the target, begin to swing the gun on the target's line, mount the gun, and shoot, all while maintaining the same swing speed for a sustained-lead shot, or a slight acceleration for a pull-away shot.

We've already seen how tiny misalignments or irregular gun movements can cause a miss, and the same is true with mounting and shooting during the swing. A sloppy mount will bobble the gun far more than a quarter inch, causing a miss by many feet. The mount phase of the swing must be smooth, with no irregular movements or misalignment between you and the gun.

It takes years to develop a smooth and consistent mount from low gun. This is one reason why more and more shooters are shifting to a semi-mounted gun. For the semi-mounted position, the recoil pad is in or near your shoulder pocket, the gun barrel just below the target line, and your head slightly raised off the stock. As the swing begins, the barrel is clearly in your peripheral vision, so you always know where it is but your vision is unobstructed. (You *never* focus on it.) A semi-mounted gun has the same advantage of unobstructed vision as the low gun without the disadvantage of gun bobble.

The last step of a swing's progression is follow-through. Follow-through means that after the shot, you continue to move the gun at the same direction and speed for a fraction of a second. Without follow-through there is no swing. Follow-through ensures you don't change the gun speed while you fire.

The single biggest reason people miss the first bird of a simo pair is because they feel rushed and cut short their follow-through. If you don't follow through, you basically stop the gun as you shoot, which removes much of the forward allowance (or lead) needed to break the target.

Swing Types

The basic swing types are swing-through (also called pull-through), sustained or maintained lead, and pull-away. With a swing-through or pull-through swing, the gun begins behind the target. With sustained or maintained lead and pull-away, the gun swing begins in front of the target.

Each type has its place in sporting clays. A proficient sporting clays shooter needs to be able to shoot all types and recognize when each type is appropriate for a given target. There are a number of minor variations of these swing types, but many of those variations are in the semantics. There's even a hybrid swing that uses swing-through and sustained lead on the same target, which can be very effective under certain circumstances.

The trick is knowing when to use each type of swing. As you preview the target, look at the amount of horizontal or vertical travel in front of

Notice how a crossing target travels from hard left to hard right, or vice-versa, in front of you.

With a quartering-away target, the bird's horizontal travel in relation to you is negligible.

you. A close or medium-distance crosser will appear to travel all the way across from hard left to hard right or vice versa.

A quartering-away target, depending on its angle, may appear to be barely moving from left to right in front of you, even though it's traveling away from you at 60+ mph. Open up the quartering target's angle from 15 degrees to 45 degrees, and its horizontal travel is still only a fraction of the total possible swing area in front of you.

Any going-away target that has a limited horizontal or vertical travel, including rising targets and driven targets, is a candidate for a pull-through swing. The limited travel is generally less than half of the total area in front of you. If the target has more horizontal or vertical travel than that, it's a candidate for sustained lead or pull-away. Pull-away is very similar to sustained lead but is reserved for longer targets.

The target's travel from hard left to hard right makes it a candidate for a sustained-lead swing. Note that the hold point is halfway between the pickup point and break point.

Hold Points

Gun hold points—the location of the gun when you call for the target—are different for each person. Effective hold points are based on your gun's weight and how it swings, how quick you are at seeing the target, and how fast your reflexes are. As a general rule of thumb for sustained lead or pull-away swing, until you develop your own feel for hold points, hold at the 50 percent position; that is, halfway between the target visual pickup point and your intended break point.

On a very slow target you could move that hold point closer to the trap, perhaps by a considerable amount. Faster targets require you to hold closer to the break point, or even to move the break point farther down the target's flight path to make sure you have enough swing room to accelerate the gun and mount into the lead and not let the target beat you.

For swing-through on quartering-away and rising targets, the less horizontal or vertical travel in relation to you, the closer your hold point should be to your breakpoint, because your swing is going to be shorter.

For all swing types, the hold point should be just below the target's line for horizontal targets like crossers or quartering targets and on the target's line for vertical and driven targets like teals, chandelles, and trap targets.

Swing-Through

Let's look at shooting a quartering-away target with swing-through. The trap is set behind the shooting station and 5 yards to the left. On a clock face, the trap is at 7 o'clock, throwing toward 12 o'clock. The shooting cage is in the center of the clock face pointing toward 12 o'clock. The trap throws a straight target about 5 feet off the ground with maximum spring—a real screamer.

First, observe the target. It screams past your left shoulder going away. At the visual pickup point—about 10 o'clock—it's just a flash of orange. Your eyes get a good focus on it at about 11 o'clock. It doesn't seem to be moving horizontally very much, but it's flying away fast, so it must need big-time gun speed, right? Wrong. The gun speed required for this shot is only slightly faster than the horizontal movement of the target in relation to you. Using the principle on swing-through hold points, our hold point should be about 11 o'clock on the clock face, and our break point will be 12 o'clock.

With a faster target, you have to move your hold point and break point far-ther down the target's flight path. This gives you more time to bring the gun up to speed and mount into the lead.

George is in his ready stance with his eyes looking left for the target.

Hold Point

George's eyes are locked on the target. As the target passes the hold point, he begins moving the gun.

This shows the dismounted position of the gun when the target passes the hold point. Note that George's face is clearly off the gun, but not by much. It doesn't need to be above the gun very far to greatly enhance visibility.

Let's take the shot. Your pre-shot routine placed you in the correct stance, with your eyes looking at 10 o'clock and your hold point at 11 o'clock. Call for the target. When you see the flash of orange to your left, follow the target with your eyes and begin moving the gun, leading with your forward hand and pivoting at the ankles while you flex your forward knee.

As soon as the target passes your barrel, come to the gun; that is, fully mount the gun as you gently swing it on the target's line. Slowly and smoothly swing through the target, firing as you pass the target at 12 o'clock.

Continue swinging the gun until about 1 o'clock to follow through. Note the ball of smoke in front of you!

Break Point

George gently swings through the target and fires. The gun swing begins with the forward hand moving the gun while the body follows from the ankles up, pivoting on the front knee.

The gun is fully mounted at the break point: face on the gun, eye perfectly aligned over the rib, full focus on the target as he controls the gun from his peripheral vision.

The most common mistake with this type of target is to hold the gun too close to the trap—in this example to hold too far to the left, at 9 o'clock or even closer to the trap. When the barrel hold point is set so close to the trap, the target seems to scream past the barrel, leading you to believe the target is getting away from you. Your immediate reaction is to sling the gun at the target to try to catch it, using far too much gun speed and causing a miss in front. By holding out in the flight path, you can use a slow, controlled swing.

If the target angle in this example was wider (the trap set a little farther to the left), the gun swing may have to pass through the target and continue for some slight distance past the target before the shot is taken.

Follow Through

George executes a distinct follow-through, continuing the front-knee pivot with shoulders square. Follow-through ensures you don't stop the gun as you fire, which reduces the forward allowance and leads to a miss behind.

Shooting with Sustained Lead

In this example, we will shoot a 30-yard right-to-left crosser at about average height. On the clock face, the shooting station is at 6 o'clock, the trap is at 3 o'clock, and our break point is at 12 o'clock.

Our target visual pickup point is at 3 o'clock, and our gun hold point is halfway between the target pickup point and the break point.

When you call for the target, your eyes should be looking at the target pickup point. When you see the flash of orange, begin to smoothly accelerate the gun along the target's intended line, guiding the gun with your forward hand, pivoting on your ankles, and flexing your forward knee. With your eyes focused on the target, continue to accelerate the gun as you mount until the desired lead

Note the pickup and hold points on this crossing right-to-left target. The gap between these two points represents the time to accelerate the gun to the targets speed. If the target feels likes it's beating you, increase this gap by moving the hold point (and break point) farther down the target's trajectory.

is visible between the barrel (in your peripheral vision) and the target. Stay synchronized with the target for a heartbeat and then shoot.

Follow through until about 11 o'clock, continuing to pivot on your ankles and flexing your forward knee. Note the large ball of smoke at 12 o'clock!

Also note the short total travel of the swing. You only swung the gun counterclockwise from about 2 o'clock to 11 o'clock. A sustained lead-type swing requires more swing distance than pull-through, but it still doesn't require a big swing. Economy of motion is very important. The more you swing the gun, the more likely you are to get into trouble with a bobble or changes in gun speed.

(continued on page 86)

This photo shows the target-barrel relationship just before the gun is fired. Note the gap between the target and the barrel—this is the lead, or forward allowance.

(continued from page 85)

The shot is taken but the gun speed never changes.

When to Use Swing-Through

Swing-through is perfect for rising targets and targets that travel short distances across, like fine-angle quartering targets. Using swing-through on crossers is problematic because of the timing. The gun travels faster than the target, so lead is generated by the difference in speeds. The forward allowance required to break the target will only be correct for a split second during the swing. Fire the gun early or late in the swing and you'll miss.

Sustained/Maintained Lead

Another primary swing type is sustained lead, also referred to as maintained lead. With this type of swing, the barrel begins in front of the tar-

As always, finish the shot with follow-through.

get and stays there. The target never gets in front of the barrel. Both of the names for this swing are misleading because they imply that once the barrel is the desired distance in front of the target and gun speed matches target speed, you somehow maintain or sustain that lead for a long period of time. Nothing could be further from the truth: When things look right, shoot.

This type of swing should be called synchronized lead instead of sustained lead. The idea is to move the gun at the same speed as the target with the barrel always in front of the target by the desired amount of forward allowance, or lead. You don't maintain this lead for any longer than it takes to make sure you have the lead right. Then you shoot without hesitation.

Remember that while you are accelerating the gun to the target speed, and while you are synchronizing gun speed with target speed, you focus on the target only. You control the barrel from your peripheral vision.

When to Use Sustained Lead

Dropping targets are perfect candidates for sustained lead because the target remains visible while you swing and mount into the lead. If you can see below your barrel when you are in battery, sustained lead can work for rising targets, too. It does not work for fine-angle quartering targets like trap shots, though, because the target does not have the horizontal or vertical movement that allows you to swing and mount into the lead.

Sustained (or synchronized) lead is an excellent swing type for typical crossing targets at any height, quartering incoming targets, and dropping targets.

In order to smoothly accelerate the gun to the target speed without any erratic movements, the gun hold point—the position of the gun when you call for the target—is· critical. You must have a significant space between where your eyes first pick up the target and the gun hold point. This space represents the time you have to smoothly accelerate the gun to the target speed.

With sustained lead, you start the swing with the gun in front of the target, accelerate the gun to match the target speed, mount into the lead, and shoot. This is the origin of the phrase "move, mount, and shoot." You must be aware of the barrel's position at all times, even before you mount the gun. Keep the barrel just below the target's line of flight as you swing and within your peripheral vision with your eyes always locked on the target.

"Mount into the lead" means that you obtain the necessary lead for the shot as you mount the gun. You should time the mount so that you are fully mounted as the correct lead is obtained. This is critical to an effective sustained-lead swing. The reason for obtaining the lead as you fully mount the gun is so your shooting brain can better evaluate the target and calculate its speed. Once the gun is fully mounted, your vision and the targeting data being fed to your brain is reduced, possibly by a large amount, depending on trajectory of the target. Your shooting brain is actually calculating the lead required even as you begin your swing and gun mount.

Gun Mount

The distance between your gun's hold point and the break point represents the time you have to accelerate the gun to the target speed and time to mount the gun. You mount the gun smoothly as you accelerate the gun, timing everything so the mount is complete at the same instant the lead fully develops. You then stay synchronized with the target for a heartbeat and then fire.

The practical application of smoothly mounting the gun between the hold point and break point means your gun mount speed is directly related to the speed of the target. If the target requires fast acceleration of the gun, it requires a fast mount.

Common Problems with Sustained Lead

The most common mistake shooters make is using a bad hold point—usually too close to the trap—causing them to rush their swing because they feel like the target has beat them. A sustained-lead swing should feel completely under control. If you feel rushed, move your hold point farther away from the visual pickup point.

Another common mistake is to slow the gun down as the shot is fired. Many shooters believe the shot is over once the gun goes off, and they lower the gun. As they shoot more, the dropping gun becomes a part of taking the shot. As we've seen, it doesn't take much erratic gun movement to cause a miss. Using a good follow-through solves the slowing and dropped gun problem.

Gun lurch as the shot is taken is another common problem with sustained lead. What should be a smooth swing becomes jerky as the gun is fired because some shooters increase their grip pressure on the gun as they pull the trigger in anticipation of recoil. This is almost like a flinch, and if not corrected it will become a flinch. It is much more likely when using sustained lead because, generally, everything is happening slower than when you are using swing-through. You should only use your trigger finger to pull the trigger, not your entire hand. Remember, smooth is paramount.

Pull-Away

Pull-away is similar to sustained lead except that instead of mounting into the lead or with the lead fully developed, on a pull-away shot you com-

Here is the gun mount as the target is launched.

plete the mount on the front of the target or some portion of the lead in front of the target with the gun speed perfectly synchronized to the target speed. Then you gently accelerate away from the target until you have obtained the desired lead and fire the gun. How far you mount in front of the target depends on the speed and distance to the target. The faster it's flying, the farther in front of it you mount. No matter how far in front you mount, the pull-away speed should only be about 5 to 10 percent faster than the target's speed. This method requires finesse and absolute control of the gun. Sustained lead and pull-away require you to synchronize gun speed and target speed. You feel the lead much better than with swing-through.

Pull-away is an advanced swing that requires a lot of practice to master. If you have mastered the ability to synchronize with a target for sustained lead, then this swing can almost completely replace the sustained-lead swing.

The gun is fully mounted just before the shot is taken.

It has the advantage of ensuring a good follow-through on the shot. As we will see in chapter 9, this follow-through becomes easy to cut short on long targets.

Hybrid Swings

Sometimes you need to use two types of swings on the same target, such as when you need to pull through a target, match speeds, mount into the lead, and then shoot. Call it a swing-through-sustained-lead method. You can use it when you are shooting a pair of targets. Killing the first target leaves the gun completely out of position for a sustained-lead shot on the second target, yet the second target is clearly a sustained-lead shot. In these cases it's best to drop the gun slightly off the shoulder while keeping the barrel tip on the second target's line; then swing through the second target, and begin mounting the gun, again timing the mount

TOM'S TAKE   So much effort goes into making a smooth and efficient stroke. I've noticed that shooters seem to shy away from lessons, but tennis players rely on pros to improve their game. And the same goes for golfers.
I highly recommend that you take lessons from a qualified instructor.

A good swing is important, and the intense focus golfers place on their swing
mirrors a good shooter's focus. Many good shooters practice their swing
indoors all year long, picking a safe, spacious room in which to swing the gun.
Mark has taught me to do this, and to always strive for smooth, efficient motion.

Mark has also taught me that mounting the gun is terribly important. I have
moved to a semi pre-mount so that my mount is a little bit smoother and not
as jerky, allowing the gun as a whole to move more smoothly and allowing me
to maintain the barrel-to-target relationship as I mount.

Mark has also taught me the importance of knowing and mastering all the
different types of swings; you will find a time to use them all.

All of which goes to say that you must find a teacher in order to improve
your game. Hang around your local club and you'll be able to figure out who can
coach. Not all great shooters are great teachers, but most great teachers are in
fact good shooters. Don't take lessons from someone who hasn't enjoyed some
success as a shooter.

with the swing so that you complete the mount as the lead on the second target fully develops. Synchronize the gun and target speed for a
heartbeat and then fire.

Common Swing Problems

A good, controlled gun swing requires finesse. It is counterproductive to
sling or muscle the gun into position.

A swing without follow-through is only half a swing. Good follow-
through ensures the integrity of the lead. Lack of follow-through eliminates lead. A jerky or bobbling gun mount will cause misses by many feet.
A smooth, consistent mount is essential to breaking targets.

A bad hold point can make you feel rushed so that you shove the gun
or swing your arm to get the gun into position. If the hold point is too
high, the gun barrel can obstruct the target. You'll never hit what you can't

see. If the hold point is too low, you may overcompensate when swinging the gun up to the target's line and miss above the target.

Shooting Subconsciously

With practice, the entire series of events we've discussed in this chapter—swing, mount, and shoot—will become subconscious. To achieve your full potential as a shooter, this process must be subconscious. As you gain experience with targets and leads, your eyes and hands will position the gun and you'll break targets without consciously thinking about each step.

All the thinking that goes into making a successful shot happens before you call for the target. Developing good form—hold point, visual pickup point, feet position, weight distribution—based on your evaluation of the target is key. This preparation gives your subconscious the maximum opportunity to break the target.

Lead

"Lead" is a term used to describe the forward allowance required to successfully break a target. You have to lead, or shoot in front of, a target because the shot strings fired from the shotgun take time to travel from the gun's barrel to the target—anywhere from .03 second for 10 yards of travel to .25 second for 60 yards of travel. (See appendix C for a 12-gauge ballistics chart.) In the time it takes the shot swarm to get to the target, the target may have moved as much as 15 to 20 feet.

To hit the target, you have to shoot in front of it, to where it's going to be, not where it's at. The farther away the target is, the farther you have to shoot in front of it, and the faster it's flying, the farther you have to shoot in front of it, too.

You might think it would be impossible to memorize every possible lead for all the target speeds and distances we see in sporting clays. In reality, it's pretty simple. First, don't try to determine actual lead; don't consider the target's distance and speed to calculate the amount of lead you need—and then try to figure out what that lead looks like over the gun barrel as you are swinging the gun.

Instead think in terms of perceived lead. Focus on the gap between the target, which has your hard focus, and your barrel, which you see from your peripheral vision. That gap represents different amounts of lead, depending on how far away the target is. The gap we

The gap you see between the barrel and the target is the perceived lead.

see between our barrel and the target represents some number of feet. How many feet it represents depends on how far away the target is.

Sustained Lead

Let's start with sustained lead, the easiest swing type with which to feel and control lead.

One of the reasons everyone sees lead differently is barrel length. Take the following example: to break a 45-mph crossing target at 20 yards, you need a 3-inch gap between your barrel tip and the target using a sustained lead swing, in which you are synchronized with the target and your gun speed equals the target speed. That 3-inch gap represents 4 feet of lead at 20 yards, which is what is required to break the target.

But you're sensing that 3-inch gap from the tip of the barrel, which could be anywhere from 28 inches to 36 or more inches from your eye, depending on the barrel and stock length. That 3-inch gap could look much bigger or smaller than 3 inches, much like any object seems to change in size based on our distance from it. The gap is still 3 inches and still represents 4 feet of lead at 20 yards, but it appears different to different people.

If you've ever used guns with varying barrel lengths to shoot skeet, you can understand why longer barrels appear to require less perceived lead to break the target. It's the same lead, but it appears smaller because the sight picture is farther from the eye.

It takes a 3-inch gap between the barrel tip and the target to break a 20-yard, 45-mph crossing target. Let's double the distance to the target to 40 yards. To break this target with a sustained-lead swing, you would think you'd have to double the gap to 6 inches, but no. This is the beauty of sustained-lead and pull-away shooting: You lead for speed, not so much for distance. The perceived lead on a 40-yard, 45-mph crosser will be slightly more than the 3-inch gap between tip and target, not double the amount. Slightly more than 3 inches, say 4 inches, because we have to account for the constantly slowing shot string. At 40 yards, a 4-inch gap between your barrel tip and the target represents about 10 feet, which is the lead required to break a 45-mph, 40-yard crosser with a shot string starting at 1200 FPS. (See appendix C.)

We know a 45-mph target takes 4 feet of lead at 20 yards distance, and that 4 feet of lead looks like a 3-inch gap between the target and the barrel. If we double the target speed to 90 mph, how much lead is required to break it now? Mathematically we can calculate from the data in appendix C that it will take 8 feet of lead to hit the target at 20 yards. If 4 feet of lead looks like a 3-inch gap between target and barrel at 20 yards, the 8 feet of lead needed for the 90-mph target will look like a 6-inch gap between target and barrel or exactly double the perceived lead for a 45-mph target. If we slowed the target down to 22 mph, we could break the target with a 1½-inch gap for 20 yards and a 2-inch gap at 40 yards.

You don't need to memorize the ballistics data if you only concern yourself with perceived lead—the relationship between barrel and target you see over your gun as you swing, mount, and shoot. If you double the target speed, you must double the perceived lead for a given distance. But if you double the distance, you only have to add about 25 percent to the gap you see between the target and the barrel.

Of the two components that determine how much perceived lead is required to break a target, speed and distance, speed has far more effect than distance on how much perceived lead is needed. Consider a 50-yard hanging teal: The target flies straight up and seems to hang for a split second before it begins to drop. As we'll see in chapter 9, you can point a perfectly still gun just below the bottom edge of this 50-yard target and hit it every time with virtually no perceived lead. No speed, no perceived lead required.

As you gain more experience shooting at moving targets and fully synchronizing your body to the target, you'll develop a feel for how much perceived lead any target takes. Remember the adage—"Lead for (mostly) speed, not (so much) for distance."

Pull-Away Leads

Pull-away leads are "felt" much like sustained leads are. Both pull-away and sustained lead require that the gun and target speeds be matched, but for pull-away, you then very gently accelerate the gun to pull away from the target as you fire. The same principles apply for pull-away and sustained lead because the leads required to break a target using pull-away are based primarily on the target's speed and secondarily on its distance.

Pull-away swing is best for leading long targets. Insert into a portion of the lead, gently accelerate the gun until the lead feels right, and shoot. This solves two problems. One is the tendency on long targets to slow the gun as you take the shot—this is called incomplete follow-through. And the other problem is the slowing pellets of the shot swarm—pull-away adds the extra forward allowance required to compensate for that. Remember that the shot swarm is slowing down from the moment it leaves the barrel of the gun until it strikes the target or falls to the ground.

Perceived leads, like hold points, look different for each shooter, so you will have to develop your own sight pictures for various target speeds. Remember, judging speeds and leads doesn't need to be perfect. Your perceived lead can be off a little because you're working with a shot swarm, not a single projectile. If you have made wise choices in your choke and ammo selection for the shot, you'll have a 2- to 4-foot pattern of shot to work with.

The perfect place to practice sustained or pull-away leads is on a skeet field. You can shoot at various-angle crossers and quartering targets and begin to develop a mental library of leads for different target angles and speeds. Keep in mind that you lead mostly for speed, so once you've mastered a fast crosser, you know that if the distance is increased, you only have to stretch the lead out a small amount.

Swing-Through Lead

Dealing with leads using the swing-through method is entirely different from pull-away and sustained lead.

In a classic swing-through shot, you fire the gun as the barrel passes through the target. All the forward allowance required to hit the target is generated by the difference in speed between the barrel and the target.

A swing-through shot can also extend past the target so that there is some perceived lead. This is similar to the perceived lead using sustained lead in that the gap between the barrel and the target represents different amounts of lead depending the distance to the target.

Swing-through is ideal for quartering-away targets and rising targets, but there are many variations of quartering-away targets. As the angle on a quartering target begins to open up, the amount of real lead required

TOM'S TAKE   I have found that sustained lead is the best way to "feel" the lead. Swing-through is a gamble—there is only one small moment in the swing when the lead is just right. A lot of shooters have trouble placing the gun in front of the target to allow for a true sustained-lead shot. That's why a good hold point is so critical.

Sustained lead was difficult at first, but I stuck with it even if I missed the bird. Once this method is mastered, I think it is the best. It is the only sure way to always be in front of the bird. It allows you to really get in sync with the bird. It does take perseverance to master. Don't give up and revert back to swing-through because you find it too difficult!

Mark taught me that one of the keys to sustained lead is to insert into the lead. I found this immeasurably helpful! Begin to swing the gun when you first see the target. Get in front of the bird and stay in front, I was taught. Get in front, stay in front, and fire when the lead feels right.

to break the target increases. It becomes closer to a crosser. To obtain that real lead, you must either swing the gun faster or swing past the target before firing.

Learning the leads for the full range of target speeds and quartering angles requires a lot of practice and consistent gun speed. For those reasons, swing-through is best for fine-angle quartering-away and rising targets where little or no swing past the target is required.

Problems with Swing-Through

One of the biggest problems with using swing-through on quartering-away targets is using too much gun speed. This can cause you to swing through and past the target in an uncontrolled manner.

Another big problem with swing-through is when new shooters rely on it for most of their shots—both quartering and crossing—and develop a paint-the-sky swing that's too big and too fast.

Swing-through is an important tool for the sporting clays shooter, but learning the leads on wide-angle quartering targets and crossing targets is more difficult than sustained lead and pull-away, which are perfect for those types of shots. With a little barrel finesse, though, swing-through is deadly on fine-angle quartering-away and rising targets.

How Much Lead?

In order to figure out how much to lead a particular target, you need to practice enough to develop a lead library, mental pictures of how much lead a target type takes at a given speed. As you synchronize your whole body to the moving target, you'll feel when the lead is right. Remember that when you swing the gun you swing it with your body from the ankles up. So when you synchronize your gun speed to the target speed, you're actually synchronizing your entire body to the target speed. This body movement synched with the target will give you the feel for lead. Practice synchronizing with targets and shooting at targets to learn which leads work.

Many shooters try to calculate the distance of the target and how many feet of lead it will take to break it. This method works sometimes, when the targets are familiar. But until you learn to synchronize your body with the target and develop an extensive lead library based on target feel, you will continue to miss a lot of targets. Trying to shoot without feeling the lead is like trying to shoot without seeing the target.

CHAPTER
7

Common Mistakes

All shooters make mistakes and all shooters miss targets because of them. This is especially true in sporting clays with its infinite variety of targets. Almost all mistakes are mistakes in form: bad hold point, bad feet position, bad visual pickup point. Some mistakes are almost universal, and these are what we'll address.

Head Off the Gun

Far and away the most common mistake new and experienced shooters make is to shoot with their head off the gun stock. This causes a miss high, the same as raising the rear sight.

The foremost reason people lift their heads while taking the shot is an improper gun fit that restricts the view of the target. When you mount the gun and are ready to fire, your eye should be correctly aligned with the rib with only light pressure between your cheek and the gun stock.

Most off-the-shelf field shotguns have very low stocks because they are intended to be used in the field where quick, unanticipated shots are the norm. With light pressure between the cheek and the stock, the only thing you can see on many guns (or on a poorly fitted target gun), is the back of the receiver. This inevitably leads you to raise your head to see the target as you take the shot.

The second most common reason for lifting the head while taking the shot is recoil. It's your body's instinctive urge to protect itself, and you move your face away from the gun as you fire. Most of the time, you don't even know it's happening.

Lifting your head from excessive recoil can usually be cured by checking gun fit, shooting lighter ammo, or changing gun types (from an over-and-under to an autoloader). If the gun's stock length is too short, the hand on the gun's wrist (specifically, the first joint of your thumb) will be jammed into your face when the gun fires and recoils. After this happens a few times, no one could keep his head on the stock—it's similar to being punched in the nose. Also, an incorrectly fitted recoil pad will concentrate recoil into a small area, magnifying its effect and causing you to lift your head.

Mark watches Tom shoot, checking for head lift, barrel-target relationship, and follow-through.

Left: *Bub has his face pressed into the gun stock as he swings on this 20-yard crosser.* **Right:** *A split second later, he raises his head and fires. To see just how far Bub has raised his head as he fired the gun, compare the height of his hat brim over the gun in these two pictures.*

A third common cause for lifting your head is poor shot setup. Selecting a hold point that is too high will cause the barrel to obscure the target, and anytime the view of the target is obstructed for any reason, you will raise your head in a effort to better see the target.

Poor setup can also lead to an arm swing. Hold too close to the trap and let the target beat you, or set up for the shot so that your body can't twist and swing as it needs to, and you're likely to shove the gun at the target with just your arms. This arm swing basically shoves the gun away from your face.

Stopping the Gun

The second most frequent mistake is stopping the gun as you fire. As with lifting your head, a number of things cause shooters to put the brakes on their swing the instant they pull the trigger. Continuing to move the gun after shooting is critical to ensure adequate forward allowance to break the target. Stopping or slowing the gun as you shoot eliminates much of the lead required to break the target, causing a miss behind.

The biggest mistake shooters make that leads to a stopped, or dead, gun is too much gun speed. That sounds counterintuitive, but it's not. On a swing-through shot with too much gun speed, your shooting brain instinctively knows the gun is moving too fast and getting too far in front of the target, and you compensate by stopping the gun as you shoot. Typically, this entire process happens in a split second. In its more subtle forms (like a sharp-angle, quartering-away target), the shooter is oblivious to the problem, and it can be quite difficult to diagnose. It is more obvious when shooting a fast crossing target. If a shooter obtains lead by using too much swing speed, the shooting brain will instinctively try to reduce the lead, resulting in a stopped gun. Often, the shooter will know he stopped the gun but not why he stopped it.

In both cases, you need to bring your gun speed under control. Start with a better hold point—one that allows more time to smoothly accelerate the gun to only the speed required and no more. Move the hold point (and break point) away from the trap and farther down the target's flight path. This has the effect of slowing the shot down and buying time for controlled acceleration.

Slowing the Gun

An improper setup is another major reason shooters change their gun speed as they shoot. Their feet are not set up to allow the gun to swing to the position they are trying to achieve. This happens frequently to experienced shooters on a report pair or simo pair of targets. You set up correctly for the first target but fail to account for the swing you are going to have to make to break the second target. Because your feet are misplaced for the second target, you slow the gun or stop the gun as you fire, resulting in a miss behind. On a long target, this can be very difficult to self-diagnose because even the slightest reduction in gun speed will cause a miss behind.

When novice shooters make this mistake, it's usually more obvious. They will set up their feet for their hold point (or even the trap itself) instead of their break point—a very common mistake. As they are swing-

TOM'S TAKE I have made every mistake in the book! I roll my shoulders. I swing too fast. I stop the gun. I fail to follow through. I bobble the muzzle like a roller coaster. I look down the muzzle and try to aim at the bird. I blow my hold points. I shoulder the gun improperly. The list goes on and on! But these are mistakes that most shooters make. What matters most is learning how to avoid these common errors. If you do, you will see your game really improve.

George tries to swing the gun left-to-right while standing flat-footed. His shoulder drops, resulting in a slower gun and a miss behind.

ing on the target, they will roll their shoulder over as they try to stay with the target, and sometimes almost fall over as they shoot. We've seen shooters so out of balance at the end of the shot that they have to take a step sideways to keep from falling. Poor form—failure to bend at the knee and twist from the feet up during the swing—will cause the same problem.

The solution to setup- and form-related problems is to take care in setting up, fully evaluating how your body must be positioned to allow you to move smoothly to both targets, and to ensure that your weight is correctly distributed on your feet and you're swinging from the feet up.

The final problem that causes you to slow the gun is lack of target focus, also known as checking lead. Your focus on the target drives the entire move-mount-shoot process. Your ability to move your gun in sync with the target is the basis for all target-breaking success and starts with a hard focus on the target. If you lose that hard focus, you will not move your gun synchronously with the target. You lose the hard focus when you focus on the rib of the gun to measure lead—you slow the gun and miss behind. Even being too aware of the rib without shifting focus to it causes a minor loss of focus on the target; with many sporting targets, that's enough to cause a very subtle loss of sync with the target, leading to a miss.

You must be aware of where your barrel is and be able to control it from your peripheral vision during the swing without breaking or diminishing your focus on the target. It takes a lot of practice to be able to focus that way effectively.

8

Mental Preparation
and Practice

porting clays is not an easy game. You are shooting at a clay target streaking through the air at a fairly high rate of speed. That target can be dipping, diving or dropping, curling, on edge, slicing, or rising. It can be crossing from left to right or right to left. Targets are launched from a tower, and some birds aren't even birds, they're rabbits!

All of this takes place in a brief moment in time on different courses on different days, in hot and cold weather, bright sunshine and overcast conditions. The variables are tremendous!

It's a thinking person's game, but when you shoot you need to stop thinking and shoot subconsciously. Shooting clays places tough demands on a shooter.

There is a lot to think about before you call for the target: foot position, hold point, focal point, break point, mount, swing, gun speed, insertion point, and the list goes on. It can be nerve-wracking.

Being in the Moment

How do you achieve that in-the-zone state of mental concentration, wherein you are vested only in the moment, only in the target, and only in the gun? How do you keep from aiming and instead relax and point and pull the trigger? Many shooters resort to a default mode: If they stumble at the beginning of a course and do poorly, they seem to forget everything they have learned and revert back to old habits, like holding back to the trap and swinging the gun wildly at the target.

Relax to Gain Control

There is a certain mental toughness required in any competitive sport. One needs the ability to focus on only one thing—the task at hand—to the exclusion of all else; the ability to compartmentalize, to put aside all the petty distractions that create mental static that will affect your game if you let them.

The key to mental toughness is to remain calm. By forcing yourself to remain calm and keep your emotions in check, you are controlling your body's reaction to those emotions.

It does no good to succumb to fear, anger, or frustration during a tournament. You're only distracting your squad mates and triggering emotional reactions in your body that will affect the way you handle the gun.

Our bodies directly reflect our emotional conditions. It's part of our physiology. Fear and anger especially cause muscle tension in the hands, arms, shoulders, and neck—the exact muscle groups that more than any others need to be relaxed to shoot well and maintain good, smooth form.

Dejection, unhappiness, and a sense of defeat have the opposite effect of anger—they remove all aggression from us. We swing the gun too slow, we approach the targets with no sharp focus, we stand flat-footed when we call for the target. Start off a tournament with a few rough stations and many shooters feel a sense of defeat and give up.

Performance Anxiety

We shoot for fun, and tournaments are a way to compete with one another, making the sport even more fun. Sporting clays organizes shoot participants into classes—Master, AA, A, B, C, D, and E. Everyone has a chance to win within their class against shooters of similar ability.

Win enough contests in your class and you advance into the next class where the process starts all over again. But tournaments can be nerve-wracking. The pressure to perform is almost always self-induced and can be overpowering.

Performance anxiety is first and foremost a fear of failure driven by a lack of confidence. You worry about a performance that hasn't even begun yet, a score for targets not yet shot. Many shooters vest a huge amount of self esteem in their shooting abilities. Some shooters are afraid that if they post a score below their expectations, that will diminish them in others' eyes.

Performance anxiety is especially fatal to good scores in a whole-body sport like sporting clays. Your mental condition affects the way you handle the gun.

Loosen Up

You know you need to be relaxed, not tense, when you call for the target and swing on it. To control the gun correctly for accuracy and consistency you must move it in a smooth, fluid manner. Too much muscle tension will cause your movements to be stiff, jerky, and uncoordinated, and you will lose fine motor control.

The solution is to have fun with each target. Remember that sporting clays is a game. You might envision it as a duel between the target setter and the shooter. Approach every station with enthusiasm, and be amazed at the

TOM'S TAKE

I rose from E to C class. I had some scores in the high 70s, even the low 80s, but then I had a tournament that really hurt. I shot a 66, and the course wasn't even that hard. I was embarrassed and humiliated, and I drove home feeling pretty sorry for myself. This has got to change, I told myself. I wanted good advice for reinventing my game. I called Mark and told him, and he was kind enough to agree to work with me on improving my shooting.

"Maybe this is the best thing to happen to you," he said. "Maybe this means you will finally listen to what I have been telling you and implement it in your game."

When I watch Mark shoot I see someone who is totally involved in the moment. He thinks before the shot and then resides only in the moment. When he calls for the target, he shifts to pure instinct. But he has preceded his call for the target with a ton of thinking about the target—how it flies and where it flies and where to shoot it.

Sporting clays is a thinking man's game as much as chess is. You must be a thinking shooter and analyze every bit of information in front of you before you call for the target.

Tom, thinking.

ingenuity and imagination of good target setters. The premier sporting clays facility in the northeast, Addieville East Farms in Rhode Island, posts a sign at every station that says, "Those who shoot to win rarely do, those who shoot for fun always win."

Breathe In, Breathe Out

Just before it's your turn to shoot, take a few deep breaths, stretch your neck, and consciously relax your shoulders, arms, and hands as you take your stance.

Stay in the moment by concentrating on the details of each target— it will take your mind off your fear and keep you from thinking about your score.

To succeed at sporting clays, you must master the details. Think about those details as you enter the shooting box and take your stance. Where's the target coming from, where do you see it, where's it going, where do you hold, where do you break it, what move do you make to the second target? Immerse yourself in the details that lead to successful breaks, and you won't have time to be anxious.

A primary mistake many shooters make is checking their score during the tournament while they are still on the course. This desire to see how you are doing reflects our outcome-based culture and is perfectly natural, but it is deadly to the focus required to perform well.

The desire to shoot well, to post a good score, itself becomes a distraction and will take you out of the moment. You focus too much mental energy on the outcome to the point that you lose focus on your target-by-target performance. And without that focus, missing targets is inevitable. So don't worry about your final score, but concentrate instead on the targets in front of you and what it will take to break them.

Sporting clays is a difficult sport that takes years to master. Don't set your sights so high you never achieve your goals. Recognize that even the greats have off-days.

Your Body, Your Mirror

Shoot with confidence. Shoot a soft-to-medium course in practice just prior to a tournament and break lots of targets to boost your confidence. In sporting clays, our bodies are mirrors of our mental state.

Anger and fear cause muscle tension, while a lack of confidence makes your approach to the target hesitant and destroys fundamental form. You

TOM'S TAKE I suffer from performance anxiety at tournaments. I get sweaty palms just driving to the course. I feel a sense of impending doom. I cannot concentrate, and if I do poorly in the beginning, the wheels come off the wagon. I forget everything I have been taught and shoot like a rank amateur.

What is worse, it takes all the fun out of the game for me. I almost always look forward to casual shooting, but frankly I dread big tournaments. I feel very nervous and full of self-doubt. I seem to feed off others' nervousness. And I particularly do not like it if I cannot warm up before the tournament begins. Mark has told me to at the very least discharge the gun a couple of times at the first station just to get the feeling of shooting.

don't swing the gun fast enough, you are likely to ride the target and measure the lead (which slows the gun down), you don't put enough weight on the lead foot, causing a shoulder-swing, a gun-shove, or worse. Controlled aggression is what breaks targets. Hesitate and you miss.

Remember these points when the jitters start on tournament day:

- Have fun—that's why you shoot.
- Relax before you call for the target.
- Stay in the moment by concentrating on the details.
- Be realistic and have reasonable expectations.
- Shoot with confidence.

How to Practice

In trap and skeet, there are only a few target presentations to master. Even with limited targets to learn, it takes at least four years for a novice shooter to become proficient enough in skeet to run his first 100 straight. That's four years of practice with coaching and shooting tournaments.

Sporting clays places far more demands on a shooter than either skeet or trap, and depending on your commitment level it may take far longer than four years to become proficient at the game.

Shooting instinctively requires hours of practice. You have to shoot enough to develop a mental target library of what type of setup, hold point, and gun swing to use for a nearly unlimited range of targets. You have to shoot at a lot of targets to begin to get the feel for target speed and distance.

You must practice the fundamentals on every shot, every time so that they become automatic. You should not have to consciously remind yourself to look back at the visual pickup point for a target before you call for it. During your pre-shot routine you should automatically evaluate the target for speed, distance, focal points, hold points, break points, foot position, and so on.

If you practice the basics on every shot, they will become automatic. But practicing bad form only reinforces bad form. To get the most from the time you spend shooting, and cut the time required to learn the game, practice in a structured manner. Simply throwing in two shells and calling pull, while certainly a lot of fun, won't necessarily improve your target-breaking abilities. In fact, without some form of oversight during your shooting, you can actually hurt your game by reinforcing bad habits. The oversight may be a friend you trust who's watching you for mistakes, a shooting coach you've paid, or even your own thoughtful evaluation after each shot.

With quality practice comes proficiency, which leads to confidence. And confidence breaks targets.

For any practice to be meaningful, you have to honestly evaluate where you are as a shooter and practice appropriately. If you can't consistently break a 25-yard crosser, don't practice on a 50-yard crosser.

Practice the basics first. When you have those mastered, move to more advanced targets.

Where to Practice

Trap and skeet fields are perfect places to practice the basics of form and swing. This is especially true of skeet, where target trajectories are known in advance.

If your local skeet and trap fields are willing to deviate from a standard round, try the following suggestions to get the most from shooting trap and skeet.

Shoot the targets as though they are all sporting targets. Don't shoot like a skeet or trap shooter, with your gun fully mounted, breaking the targets very early as they do. Shoot with your usual sporting gun mount, taking care to set up for a realistic break point. You'll get some strange looks from the skeet and trap crowd, but the idea is to practice setup and a solid move-mount-shoot technique. For sporting shooters, these targets are far simpler than the usual sporting clays targets, giving you a chance to really focus on form.

Henry Trial's 5-Stand Setup

At the Hermon Skeet Club, Henry Trial has devised a unique way to shoot 5-stand that more closely resembles sporting clays. It is fantastic practice. Henry starts with eight traps. He assigns two traps to each station so that every target shot from each station comes off the same two traps. He has a flexible controller that allows him to automate shot rotation, and he made printed menus to eliminate confusion. He shoots either a 30- or 50-target round, either three pairs or five pairs of targets from each station. Shooter rotation remains the same. Each shooter shoots a pair in turn, either report or simo. After the designated number of pairs, shooters rotate until all shooters have fired from each cage.

Henry's system is excellent for serious practice because you have the opportunity to refine each shot and work on tough pairs. You may miss, but you'll have the opportunity to evaluate, make adjustments, and try again with the exact same target. It's also good practice for learning to duplicate your setup and swing on tough targets.

Do repetition drills. Shoot the same target repeatedly, breaking it in exactly the same place each time. Break a skeet station low 2 target six times exactly over the center pin. Then change foot position and hold point and break it six times in a row 20 feet past the center pin.

One of the more difficult things a sporting shooter has to be able to do is break a particular target in a specific spot (not always the sweet spot) so the gun is in the correct place for the second target of a report or simo pair. Repetition drills on a skeet field are great for teaching yourself the trigger control required to precisely control your break point.

If your local trap and skeet fields allow it, step off the shooting stations to get more of an angle and more distance to the target (left and right on a trap field and behind on a skeet field). This should always be done safely and according to club rules.

You can also practice on reentry targets after an NSCA tournament. Most clubs hosting NSCA tournaments will allow you to reshoot the course for a reduced fee. This is a perfect opportunity to go back to particular stations that may have caused you some problems and figure out those pesky targets.

If you have the opportunity to set up your own 5-stand, you can practice particular target presentations that give you problems or that you're curious about. You can set up reports and simo pairs tailored to your skill level.

Another valuable practice strategy for trap, skeet, or 5-stand is to practice shooting targets early and late. By their nature, some simo and report pairs force you to either break a target earlier than you want to if you want any chance at the second target, or break a target much later than you normally would. Be ready for those situations by practicing early and late breaks in a structured practice session. One of the practice techniques we use on a skeet field is to stand 5 yards behind station 6, and then throw a low house target, shooting at it as it drops about 65 yards away. It's amazing how little lead you need because it's travelling so slowly. It's great fun and great practice.

The single most important thing you'll learn by practicing is to correctly evaluate why you missed a target. It's critically important that you be able to evaluate a miss, figure out what corrections to make, and reshoot— and break—the target. You should constantly evaluate yourself after each shot. If the target beat you and you felt rushed, move the hold point and break point out a little. Or if you rolled your shoulder and pulled the gun offline a little or were off balance at the end of the shot, move your feet so you have more room to swing the gun.

You should go through this evaluation process for each and every shot, constantly making adjustments as required. That's how you improve— structured practice with thoughtful self-evaluation.

Target Types
and Strategies
to Break Them

In sporting clays, you shoot a single target, targets on report (the second target launches on the report of the gun on the first shot), and simultaneous pairs, also called simos or doubles. Shooting a single target in flight is pretty basic, and the rules allow you to shoot at it twice. Reports and doubles are another matter.

Problems you might have with report pairs are not getting the gun into the right position for the second target or not looking at the second target's visual pickup point. With a true pair, when two targets are launched at once, it's easy to become visually confused by the sudden introduction of not just one but two targets in the sky.

Often a dramatic move is required from one target to the next. When two targets are flying in the same direction, it can be difficult for the eye to pick out one to shoot at first.

The trick to breaking report pairs or simo pairs is planning. You must plan every move you're going to make on both targets in advance. Pay close attention to the targets during preview and know where your visual pickup points, hold points, and break points are going to be for both targets. Visualize the moves you're going to make.

Set up your stance for the second target's break point. Sometimes this will make things a little awkward for the first target, but that's the nature of the game (and probably the way the target setter planned it!).

For report pairs, you must identify the second target's hold point and visual pickup point before you call for the first target. You need to move your gun to the second target's hold point as soon as possible after the first shot. You may need to adjust your first target's break point in order for your gun to be in the correct position for the second target. The single biggest mistake people make with report pairs is not getting their gun to the correct hold point for the second shot.

Think of it like a game of pool. Half of the challenge of pool is getting the cue ball where you want it after the first shot so you are set up for the follow-up shot. Same with a report pair in sporting clays.

On simo pairs, you usually don't need to rush the second shot if you plan things carefully, even though you may feel you'll need to rush when you first see the targets. As a general rule, take the lowest of the two targets first. This will generally buy you time for the second target.

Again, think of the pool game and positioning the cue ball. Plan your break point on the first target so you leave yourself in the best possible position to start your swing on the second target.

When transitioning from the first target's break point to the second, don't rush or you will blow by the second target. Make your move in a controlled and smooth fashion—the transition move is the start of your swing on the second target.

If your gun has only one choke, choke for the farther target. If you practice breaking targets both early and late, you'll give yourself many more options on report and simo pairs.

There is an almost infinite number of target presentations in sporting clays—unlike skeet and trap—making it hard to paint a picture of a typical sporting clays target. But there are some basic types, described below.

Crossers

Crossers fly out in front of you, parallel to your station, left to right or right to left and at almost any distance from 5 yards to 75 yards—although 75 yards is an extreme target presentation. They may be moving very fast, as much as 70 mph with the new sporting biodegradable targets, which doesn't leave you much time to shoot them.

Shoot crossers with a sustained-lead swing or a pull-away swing. For sustained lead, start in front and stay in front, synchronize the gun speed to target speed on the target's line as you mount the gun, mount into the lead, stay synchronized with the target for a heartbeat, and shoot when the lead feels right. Don't hesitate or measure the lead. Keep a hard focus on the target and control the barrel from your peripheral vision. Keep your head on the gun and execute a smooth follow-through.

For pull-away, follow the sustained-lead sequence above but instead of mounting into the full lead, mount into a portion of the lead, depending on the speed and distance to the target, and then gently accelerate away from the target on the target's line no more than 5 to 10 percent of the target's speed. When the lead feels right, fire without hesitation.

Advanced Technique for Long Crossers

Long crossers—crossing targets beyond 40 yards—present a special challenge. The farther a target is from you, the slower it appears to be moving, much like a jet airliner that flies 5 miles above you at 500 miles per hour but appears to be nearly motionless in the sky. When the gun is synchronized with a long target, it may be barely moving. This slow gun movement makes it too easy to stall the gun as it's fired or not execute a good follow-through, especially when using a sustained-lead swing. Either of those errors can easily cause a miss.

The solution is to use a pull-away swing. You insert into most of the lead, gently pull away on the target's line until the lead feels right, and then shoot. This technique keeps you from slowing the gun as you fire and ensures good follow-through. To use this technique effectively, you must have absolute control of your gun. Pull-away is executed with only about 5 to 10 percent more speed than the speed of the target. To do that correctly takes a lot of practice.

Trap-Type Targets

Trap-type targets, so called because they are similar to the targets thrown in the game of trap, are usually thrown from in front of the shooter with some slight upward and sometimes right or left trajectory. They are often long targets, requiring finesse, a powerful shell, and a lot of choke.

Trap-type target presentation.

Many shooters use a fully mounted gun on this target, much like trap shooters do. To break these targets, your hold point should be on the target's line and just above the trap. When the target rises above the barrel, gently swing the gun up to the target and fire as the barrel covers the target. It is critical not to use too much gun speed on the swing up or you will miss high. Gentle gun movement is key. This target usually flies very fast. In order not to feel rushed, and because it's mostly an edge presentation, use plenty of choke and a 7½ shot shell suitable for handicap trap distances. If you find yourself missing these high (and you'll know!), move your hold point up. This will reduce the amount of upward movement required to bring the barrel to the target and make it less likely that you'll swing past the target.

Trap-Teal Variations

The trap-teal variation of a trap-type target is set to throw high. At first glance it looks like a springing teal target—with one significant difference. The trap-teal variant does not rise as fast as a true teal because it's not only going up but also away at a high rate of speed. This subtle difference leads to many misses over the top of this target. In fact, a close examination of the target trajectory shows that it rises quickly for the first half of its ascent, but then its rate of rise slows quickly until it peaks out and begins dropping.

These are usually very long targets requiring a subtle gun swing. Shoot them using swing-through as with the trap-type target. Hold about halfway between the trap and the target's highest point, directly on the target's line. When the target rises above your barrel, mount the gun just behind it and gently swing through it using minimum gun speed. Generally, firing the gun just as you pass the target is all the forward allowance these targets need. As with the trap target, if you find yourself missing these targets high, move your hold point up slightly to reduce the gun speed as you swing up to the target.

Advanced Technique for Trap and Trap-Teal

An alternative method of breaking the trap and trap-teal targets is to use a sustained-lead swing above the target while looking below your barrel. Just like sustained lead for a crosser, the idea is to hold far enough above the trap so that the target does not beat you or get ahead of the barrel. When the target launches, mount your gun as you start your swing ahead of the target on its line. When the lead feels right, fire as you continue the swing upward.

This technique presumes you can see the trap below your barrel. One-eyed shooters or shooters wearing a patch will have difficulty seeing the trap. Also, depending on your gun's shape, where you place your hand on the fore-end, and even what clothes you are wearing, looking below the barrel may not work for you. But if you can see below the barrel, this is an excellent way to break any of the trap-type targets.

Springing Teal

This target rises straight up and is an all-around challenge, whether you try to shoot it on the way up, at the top, or when it is dropping.

Springing teal out to about 40 yards are easiest shot on the way up using swing-through, or at the peak. To shoot them on the way up, carefully mark the point where you first see the target and how high it goes. Hold directly over the trap in the target's flight path and about halfway to the target's highest point.

Call for the target with your eyes looking directly over the barrel. You'll see the target appear over your barrel traveling upward. Gently and smoothly swing the gun upward through the target, mounting the gun as you swing. (This technique works best from a semi-mounted gun.) Swing through the target and fire just after you pass the target.

This is a leap-of-faith shot because the target seems to disappear as you swing past it. Don't swing too far past the target before you fire and don't swing the gun too fast.

The classic rising or springing teal.

Fire just as the hanging teal begins to drop, pointing at the bottom edge of the target.

Complete the shot with a smooth follow-through and observe the smoke ball hanging in the sky in front of you.

Any springing teal, but especially long teal at or beyond 40 yards, is best shot at the hang; that is, at the point of highest travel, just before it begins to fall. A true springing teal moving straight up will appear to hover for a split second before it begins to drop. That is when you should shoot it with a dead gun, or a gun with no movement in any direction. Pointing the gun just below the target is all the lead this target requires. Using this technique, it's easy to break teal targets out to 75 yards and beyond.

Advanced Techniques for Springing Teal

Like trap-type targets, if you can see below your barrel, using sustained lead on a rising teal target works very well. Your hold point should be high enough above the trap so that the target doesn't beat you. When you see the target launch, begin swinging your gun up, mounting into the lead when the lead is right. Fire the gun as you continue your swing upward. In general, a springing teal shot this way will require more lead than a trap-teal because it's rising faster.

Dropping Teal

You can easily find yourself having to break the teal as it drops when it's in a simo pair. This is not a particularly difficult shot, even though many shooters shy away from it. Hold just below the high point of the teal's trajectory. Wait for the target to peak and begin to drop. While staring at the target, move the gun down and begin the mount on the target's line as it drops, inserting into the lead.

A valuable technique for this target is to move with it for a few heart-beats longer than usual. The target is usually well above the barrel, so the

A dropping teal.

rib is not likely to draw the eye. With your face solidly on the gun, fire as you continue to swing downward. You must be solidly on the gun or you'll miss high. You must also finish the shot with a distinct follow-through—sometimes referred to as "bowing to the target."

If the target is very high, you should start the swing with most of your weight on your back foot, shifting your weight to your front foot as you swing down. Remember to continue to swing downward after you fire.

For a dropping teal past 40 yards, use a pull-away swing to ensure you don't stall the gun as you fire.

Off-Angle Teal

A frequently seen target is the off-angle rising teal. It's not going straight up but instead is angled slightly to the right or left. It is an easy-to-miss target because it can require an awkward move to stay on the target's line as it rises. Cant the gun in your hands just enough so the rib is perpendicu-

The off-angle teal shot on the rise. Note the canted gun so that the rib is perpendicular to the trajectory.

lar to the target's line. It's also helpful to slightly cant your shoulders and upper body so that you can smoothly move on the target's line as you swing through the target.

Advanced Technique for Off-Angle Rising Teal

As with straight-up teals and trap-type targets, if you can see below your barrel, sustained lead is a great way to break this type of target. The canted gun and upper body still apply, but look below your barrel for the target. When it launches, begin swinging the gun up on the target's line, inserting into the lead. Fire when the lead is right as you continue to swing up.

Rabbit

The rabbit is a target unique to sporting clays and a lot of fun to shoot. A rabbit target, a solid disk of a target with a reinforced edge, rolls across the ground like a wheel. It is made much tougher than any other target used

The rabbit target is unique to sporting clays.

in sporting clays so that it can survive bouncing on the ground. It is an extremely unpredictable target because it may roll over a broken target piece or other object on the ground, bouncing into the air unexpectedly and possibly even changing trajectory. It is almost always going slower than it appears because it is so close to its background.

To break a rabbit, make sure you use your heaviest shell with plenty of choke. It can be difficult to break because it is so tough. If you are unsure of the correct lead, shorten it. It doesn't take as much as you think. If you have a hard focus on a rabbit target and it bounces while you're swinging on it, you will automatically correct and hit it.

Most rabbits are below your horizon, so use the aggressive stance, keeping most of your weight on your lead foot and your front knee slightly more bent. This helps keep your head on the gun during the swing. (See the setup chapter for more on the aggressive stance.) You'll miss targets below your horizon high if your face is even a little loose on the gun stock.

Shoot rabbit targets like standard targets. If they are crossing, they are candidates for sustained lead. If they are finer angle quartering, they are perfect for swing-through.

Overhead

The overhead tower target typically flies from overhead and behind you, either going straight out or diving. It may be launched from your left or right or even directly overhead. You almost always see a version of this target at a tournament.

Take this target with a sustained-lead or pull-away swing. Your hold point should be on the target's line and far enough down its flight path so it does not beat you. Your eyes should look up as high as is practical so you can smoothly accelerate the gun and insert into the lead.

This type of target does not require much gun movement. Depending on how much the target is dropping, your hold point should be very near your break point.

On any dropping target, (even one coming from over your head) solid contact between your face and the gun stock is critical. This target is no exception—even though it may be far over your head, it's still a dropping target. If you're loose on the gun, you'll miss over the target.

Follow-through is especially critical for any dropping target, although in general the overhead target won't require a big follow-through because the total gun movement is usually fairly small.

The overhead going-away target.

Quartering Away

A quartering away target flies away from you at an oblique angle. It's another target that seems to fly extra fast, leaving little time to break it.

When a quartering-away target presents a fine going-away angle (and is almost straight away), hold near your break point. Let the target pass your barrel, and then gently swing through the target, firing the gun as you pass the target.

On wider angle quartering-away targets, use sustained lead or pull-away. The basic principles regarding lead apply here as with crossers.

Quartering Incomer

The quartering incomer flies toward you at almost any angle or height and generally lands in the area in front of the shooting cage. It is perfect

The quartering-away target. Minimum gun movement and a hold point close to the break point are the keys to success with this target type.

for sustained lead or pull–away, as long as you understand that because of the approach angle, not as much perceived lead is required as compared to an equivalent speed crosser.

This is also a good target type for mounting and shooting as late as possible. With this target, you usually see it for a long time before you shoot it. Do not mount the gun as soon as you see the target and track it across the sky. Keep your gun at its hold point and watch the target come to you. It is much easier to maintain a hard focus on the target if the gun is not in your face.

When the target approaches your hold point, gently accelerate the gun, staying in front of the target as you smoothly mount into the lead. Stay syn–chronized for a heartbeat and then shoot. Depending on the target's

Quartering incomer.

approach angle, this may be a minimum-movement shot, or it could be almost like a crosser.

Incoming Floater

The incoming floater comes almost straight toward you and hangs in the air. People often miss it because they don't understand the principle of leading for speed, not for distance.

If the target is barely moving horizontally and coming almost directly at you, it doesn't need much lead. If it's hovering slowly above the ground, it's barely moving and doesn't need much lead either. Seeing a small amount of daylight between the target and the barrel is all the sustained lead this target requires. Use a gentle gun movement when swinging on this target.

The ammunition you use on this target is important because the target is usually at the very end of its flight. It has very little velocity or centrifugal (spin) energy, so no other forces help break it apart. For that reason you should use a heavy shell with 7¹/2 shot for this target regardless of its distance.

Chandelle

From the French word for candle, the chandelle goes up, over, and down in a flight trajectory that forms a perfect arc. The term chandelle describes a target trajectory, not a unique type of target. Any of the target types used in sporting clays can be launched to fly as a chandelle, even a rabbit target. There are many different chandelle presentations: high trajectory, flat trajectory, crossing, quartering in, and quartering away. The chandelle can be

Crossing high chandelle. Minimum, very smooth gun movement is the secret to breaking this target.

shot as it rises, at the top, and as it drops. Originally, chandelles were launched from a specialty trap similar to a rabbit trap but turned upward to throw the target into the air. In these machines, the target launches upright and stays in this orientation as it flies through its arc. However, newer generation all-purpose sporting traps can tilt sideways enough so they can throw a very similar target except it flies in a lopsided arc trajectory instead of a perfect arc. For the purposes of this discussion, all of these target trajectories are grouped together as chandelles.

Fire on the crossing high chandelle just as the target rolls over and begins to drop, using sustained lead or gentle pull-away. Instead of consciously applying a compound lead to this target, look for the target's line as it rolls over and use a gentle sustained-lead swing or pull-away to synchronize gun speed with the target. Mount into the lead when it feels

Flat crossing chandelles generally require more lead, as these targets are traveling fast.

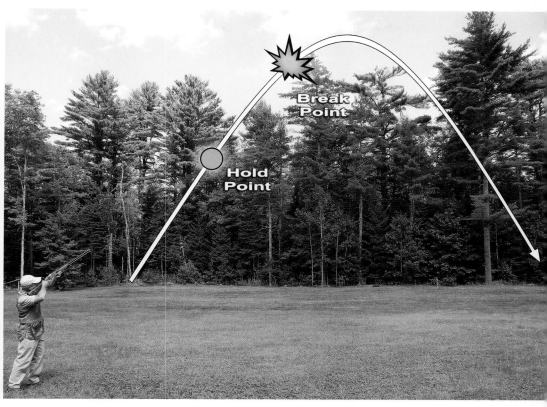

A quartering-away chandelle should be shot on the way up, just before the target peaks.

right and fire with a distinct follow-through. You need finesse, not a big swing. Note how close the hold point is to the break point in the picture. Gentle gun movement is the rule for this type of target.

If you are using pull-away, insert just in front of the target and gently pull away on the target's line until the lead feels right; then shoot.

For a crossing flat chandelle, sustained lead and pull-away are still the best options, but it's best to fire on the target at the top of its flight path, instead of at the rollover point. Flat chandelles are generally moving fast, so they will take far more lead than the high, arcing chandelle, which may appear to stall in the air at the top of the arc.

A quartering-away chandelle is usually best fired on using swing-through on its way up before it peaks. Depending on the quartering-away

An incoming chandelle is best shot as it drops.

angle, you may need to hold just inside the line of the target as it rises. Swing on the rising chandelle just as you would swing on a rising trap–teal target.

A quartering incoming chandelle either high or flat is best fired on just past the top of the arc, at the rollover point as the target begins to drop. As with all dropping targets, your head must be firmly anchored on the gun. This is a minimum movement shot, usually with a short swing. Sustained lead is perfect for this type of shot. In order to break this target consistently, you need a distinct follow–through on the target line.

Dropping Targets

Droppers can be challenging presentations. You don't see dropping targets in any other shotgun sport; they are unique to sporting clays. Many shooters have difficulty with dropping targets because they don't use the proper form and because there are as many dropping target speeds as there are different target trajectories. Correct body movement and weight shift are critical for success with these targets. When a dropper is the second target of a pair, it can be even more difficult because you have very little time to find the target's line and lead before it hits the ground. You need to know how to shoot droppers both early and late.

You'll see dropping targets more and more often in sporting clays. Sometimes they drop slowly, almost hovering as they fall dome-up, like a helicopter landing, or they can fall on edge, accelerating faster and faster as they fall. Different target types fall differently, too. A battue target or a flying rabbit on the drop have little wind resistance, so they accelerate quickly. A standard 108-millimeter target, because of its construction, has a lot of wind resistance, even dropping on edge, so it won't accelerate as fast as a battue or rabbit.

There are a few basic shooting principles common to all dropping target presentations. Your face must be solidly on the gun. A loose touch on the comb, and you'll miss the target high.

You must execute a distinct follow-through as you fire. Many shooters find that a slow pull-away works for them. Your downward swing should be accompanied with a shift in weight to your forward foot as you swing so that you end up with nearly all your weight on your forward foot.

Sustained lead, with perhaps a slight amount of pull-away, is always the best way to shoot a dropping target. Insert into the lead as you swing down, fire the gun, and follow through with a distinct downward move, shifting your weight to the forward foot as you swing. Don't just dip the muzzle

TOM'S TAKE

I had fits with the chandelle. Box after box after box I shot away, trying to master this shot. I think I must have missed a hundred times straight. No matter where I placed the gun I missed—I couldn't even get one lucky shot! But I learned some important things. One, shooting and shooting and shooting without a good coach helping you does more harm than good. Two, you must have a plan! In this case follow-through is everything.

I try not to get discouraged when I struggle. I can hit the chandelle now, but it took a long time to even begin to improve on this shot. Remember, this can be a tough game!

A high dropping target requires a gentle grip, weight on the back foot, and head off the gun, ready to insert into the lead and ride the target down.

Take the shot with your face solidly on the gun; all the weight has shifted forward as the target has dropped.

as you fire but continue to move the gun downward with your whole body, bowing to the target. Because you lead for speed and not for distance, and because there are so many different speeds for dropping targets, this type of target presentation takes an enormous amount of practice to master. Generally, if you use good consistent form, droppers don't take as much lead as you think.

Driven Targets

This target presentation has its roots in the beginning of the sport—the English driven bird shoots. In these shoots, a line of beaters would flush—or drive—upland birds toward waiting shooters. The birds would fly fast and high, usually over the shooters' heads.

This is a target trajectory that isn't seen too often anymore because target pieces can fall on shooters or spectators. Typically, a driven target now

The driven target is based on English upland bird shoots.

George swings on a driven target. All of his weight is on his back foot.

has some left or right deflection to it so it doesn't fly directly over you, but the basic idea of a bird flying fast and high toward you is still preserved.

There is a very simple way to shoot this type of target—exactly like a rising teal with swing-through. Your hold point should be slightly above and directly in line with where the target first appears. Let the target rise above your barrel, mount the gun just behind the target, and gently pull through the target. Use finesse—not too much gun speed. For slow- and medium-speed targets, fire as you pass them. The faster the target, the farther past the target you should swing before you fire. With practice, you'll soon feel how far past the target you have to swing based on its speed and distance.

Your weight distribution is important. As you swing on the target, shift your weight to your back foot. You typically finish the shot with the gun pointing nearly straight up with all your weight on your back foot.

Battue

The battue is a specialty target unique to sporting clays. It is 108 millimeters, like the standard dome, but it is nearly flat and only about a quarter-inch thick.

When launched upward, it flies flat like a dome target, but because it's so thin, it's very difficult to see. When it peaks, it rolls over, showing its full face to the shooter. Because it's so hard to see when rising, it is usually shot as it drops. Your hold point should be near the peak of its trajectory. As the target rolls over and shows its face, you should swing the gun downward

TOM'S TAKE While the target setters try to make difficult presentations in tournaments, the basic types of targets are easy to enumerate. Make sure you practice them all.

Practice at a course where you can repeatedly attempt a particular type of target. If you are struggling to master a rabbit, then get out there and hammer away at the rabbit.

An important lesson Mark taught me is to try something different if you are missing. Do not attempt the same shot over and over again if it is not working. Try a little more front, or a little less, a different swing—anything, just don't keep repeating the same mistake!

The battue target's trajectory is unique because of the flat shape of the target.

The camera perfectly catches the instant the shot swarm hits the target and starts to tear it apart.

on the target's line, inserting into the lead. Maintain the lead for a heartbeat and then fire, continuing the swing downward. As with all dropping targets, you need to keep your face on the gun stock and follow through with your upper body. Depending on how high the target flies, you may have to shift your weight significantly to the front foot as the target drops. For long battues, use a pull-away swing so you don't stall the gun as you fire.

Battue targets can be especially difficult because often they are invisible to the shooter until they have reached their apogee and rolled over, exposing their face and becoming visible. From the shooter's point of view, they seem to magically appear out of thin air just as they begin their drop. When you see a battue presentation like this, don't panic. Smoothly move the gun to the front of the target, pull away to get the lead on the target's line, mount and shoot without hesitation, and complete the shot with a distinct follow-through.

Tournaments: The National Sporting Clays Association

The NSCA is the national governing body for competitive English sporting clays and FITASC in the United States and Canada. It establishes the rules and regulations of the sport and manages classes and punches.

There are three categories of competition at most NSCA tournaments: open, concurrent, and class. Open competition determines the tournament champion, runner-up, and possibly third, based on the size of the shoot. Everyone who enters the tournament is eligible and competes for the open category.

The concurrent categories are age- and gender-based classifications that allow competition between shooters of similar demographics. There's a sub-junior and junior concurrent category for those 21 and younger, a ladies concurrent, and three categories of veteran concurrent for anyone 55 or older. As the name implies, competition among shooters in these groups occurs concurrently with the class and open competitions.

There are seven classes that rank shooters of similar abilities. Master is the highest class, followed by AA, A, B, C, D, and E.

As an example, a 56-year-old male in A class enters a large tournament, competing for the open award. He also competes against all other 55- to 64-year-old veteran concurrent participants and against everyone in A class. At most shoots, there are separate awards for open, concurrent, and class champions.

The basic measure of shooting ability in the NSCA is the class assignment, and you advance through the classes by winning class awards in tournaments. The higher your class, the greater your shooting proficiency. When you start, you are usually assigned to D class. If you have been a member of other clay target organizations like the ATA or NSSA for trap and skeet, you may be assigned a higher NSCA starting class. Each year an annual review is conducted, and based on your performance you may be downgraded to a lower class. You can refuse the downgrade and elect to participate in a higher class (up to AA class) by declaring into the class for the entire shooting year. You cannot declare into Master class—that must be earned through the accumulation of punches.

You earn your way up through all the classes with punches. One or more punches are awarded when you place first in class—or second or third, depending on how many are shooting in the class at the event. A different number of punches are required at each step up the ladder. It takes six punches to move from C to B class and sixteen to move from AA to Master. You have two years to accumulate punches for a move to a higher class. See Appendix D for a complete breakdown of the punch system.

As the governing body of the sport, the NSCA sanctions official tournaments. Each year a complete list of these shoots is compiled and posted on the NSCA website. Normally, you pre-register for large shoots at the hosting club's website and pay a fee for the events you sign up for.

There are different scoring options you can choose from. For example, some shooters like to opt for entry into the Lewis class event, which is based on final scores. Prior to the event, the shoot promoter decides the number of Lewis classes and the payout per class, such as one class per 15 shooters, two or three payouts per class. When the shoot is over, scores are listed numerically from highest to lowest. Then they are divided into as many groups as there are Lewis classes. For example, if there are 30 entries and five classes, there will be six scores in each class. The highest score in each Lewis class is the winner.

There are also class options, a sort of side bet where you bet on yourself. The winner is the shooter who posts the best score in that class of all those who choose to play the class option.

Tournaments can draw hundreds of shooters. Usually, there is also a 5-stand competition, which is a good warm-up for the main event. Also common are one or more preliminary events (smaller versions of the main event), a long bird contest, a game called Make A Break, and FITASC.

It's also common for there to be a vendor's row where you can buy all sorts of things, from vests to guns. There are also usually a number of good gunsmiths who can perform on-site repairs.

Tournaments, big and small, also afford you a chance to observe good shooters and study their form. At the really big shoots, you can see some of the best shooters in the world. Some tournaments use a European start, which means you can start and finish at any time of your liking. Other starts are more strictly regimented. You may be assigned a particular station to start at and a specific time to be there. At large shoots, each station has a referee.

In addition to the big shoots with many hundreds of competitors, there are many NSCA-sanctioned local shoots almost everywhere in the United States.

Another important function of the NSCA is selecting members to state, zone (regional), and national teams. These are merit-based selections and are considered a singular honor and the high point of many shooting careers.

The NSCA sanctions annual state championships, zone championships, and the U.S. Open and national championship. You can earn points for open, class, and concurrent categories for state and zone teams, and open and concurrent categories for All-American teams.

The NSCA also selects members to Team USA, the shooting team that represents the United States in international competition in English sporting clays and FITASC. The selection process is separate from state, zone, and All-American teams and is based on performance at a series of selection shoots determined by the NSCA. The annual points races for all team selections are on the NSCA website at www.mynsca.com. The NSCA website is an incredible resource for all shooters. It contains all the rules, the latest news, every member's shooting record, and contact information and schedules for every member club. Imagine you are planning a cross-country trip and you would like to shoot a little at your destination. You can search the schedules database for your destination city or state and get a list of available clubs and tournaments for the times you are interested in. The website can even give you driving directions to the clubs you want to visit.

Every sporting clays shooter should join the National Sporting Clays Association. It's the only way to really participate in all the aspects of the game, and it is the best way to support your sport. An annual membership—which makes you a registered shooter—costs $40 and you also get access to their website and a subscription to *Sporting Clays* magazine. However, for those who want to get a taste of the game but have not yet joined the NSCA, there is a hunter class for non-NSCA members. It's designed to allow new shooters to participate in organized shoots. Hunter class is administered by the hosting club. Generally, hunter class participants win small awards based on the Lewis class description above.

Equipment

Sporting clays demands much more from the equipment than the other clay target disciplines. The distances, the varied shooting conditions, and the enormous variety in target presentations means if you expect to reach your shooting potential, your equipment has to work. This is true of the guns, ammo, chokes, glasses, even the clothes we wear (you don't want to wear a jacket that keeps you from pointing the gun straight up). As a result, sporting clays has developed into an "equipment" game. There are hundreds of vendors of shooting-related equipment targeting the sporting clays community for potential customers. This is fantastic for shooters because it gives us a huge assortment of things to choose from. But not all items work as advertised or work well under the unique conditions presented by our sport.

The list of recommendations of the equipment that has worked best for us represents many years of shooting and hundreds of thousands of rounds downrange.

Gun

TOM: The Krieghoff K-80. Mine has the new lightweight 32-inch barrels and titanium screw chokes.

MARK: The Beretta 391. The best pointing shotgun I've ever owned, light and well balanced with low recoil. I shoot a release trigger.

Gunsmith

TOM: Chris and Audrey Maest of Clay Target Sports, Inc., in Princeton, New Jersey. (609) 921-9358. Also a very good place to buy a Krieghoff. Todd Beinhauer—another very good gunsmith—works for them.

MARK: Cole's Gunsmithing in Harpswell, Maine, (207-833-5027) and Howell's Gun Shop in Gray, Maine, (207-657-2324) are great places to buy Beretta guns and Beretta accessories. They both have fully qualified Beretta gunsmiths on staff.

Barrel and Choke Shop

MARK: Briley Manufacturing in Houston, Texas. (713) 932-6994. Briley's thin-wall chokes for the Krieghoff are, dollar for dollar, the best investment in performance you can make for your shotgun.

In my opinion, Pure Gold chokes for the Beretta 391 are the best after-market choke available. I use their spreader choke for close targets.

Ammo

TOM: I like Remington Light Target Loads in 8 for almost everything except rabbits and long targets, when I switch to Nitro 27 in $7^1/2$. I always use $1^1/8$ ounces of shot.

MARK: For tournaments, I only use premium ammo: Federal or Remington STS 3 dram $1^1/8$-ounce 8 shot or Fiocchi White Rhino in 8 for in close, and Remington Nitro 27 or Winchester AA Super Handicap for long targets, both in $7^1/2$ shot. For FITASC, I use Fiocchi Crushers in $7^1/2$. For practice and play I use almost anything.

Stock Shop

TOM: I am happy with the stock that came standard on my K-80, a Sporting #3.

MARK: From a custom stock to recoil pads, adjustable combs, and any other type of stock work, Bud's Gun Stocks in Rye, New Hampshire, is the place to go. (603) 964-6600.

Places to Shoot

TOM: Sarasota Trap, Skeet & Clays in Nokomis, Florida, is where I shoot in the winter. (941) 488-3223. I also recommend Addieville East Farm, in Rhode Island, a truly stellar facility. They can be reached at (401) 568-3185.

MARK: Hermon Skeet Club near Bangor, Maine, throws the best sporting targets in northern New England. (207) 394-2655.

The L. L. Bean 5-stand in Freeport, Maine, is a great place to shoot easy to moderate difficulty targets. (888) 552-3261. A new sporting clays facility in Scarborough, Maine, is becoming very popular because of its excellent tournaments—well run with great targets. It's the Scarborough Fish and Game Club's sporting clays program (207-839-2364).

The Arnold Trail Gun Club in Sidney, Maine, is simply the best small shooting club in America. It has everything, including unlimited access to members for trap, skeet, and 5-stand. They can be reached at arnoldtrail@roadrunner.com.

For the very best of the really large shoots and a chance to see the All-Americans compete, M & M Sporting Clays in Pennsville, New Jersey, (856-935-1230) is the place to go.

Reprinted with permission of Gil Ash.

B R I L E Y
A Legacy of Shooting Innovation.
800.331.5718
www.briley.com

GIL & VICKI ASH
**OPTIMUM SHOTGUN
PERFORMANCE
SHOOTING SCHOOL**
800-838-7533
www.ospschool.com

Briley Extended Chokes to exact constrictions were
used in researching the information in this choke chart
If the choke in your gun is not to exact constrictions,
your results may be slightly different.
© 2003 Gil Ash / OSP Shooting School

Choke Selection

Choke selection for sporting clays should not be determined by distance alone. Three things need to be considered:

1. **Target Presentation** –
How much surface area is presented to the shooter?

2. **Target Vulnerability** –
How easy is that surface to break?

3. **Target Distance** –
At what distance will the target be broken?

Target Profiles

Easiest to Break

Belly On
14.2 sq. in.
Approx.

Back Lip

Hardest to Break

Edge On
3.65 sq. in.
Approx.

Dome On

These two profiles are *easiest* to break.

The **belly on** profile offers not only the largest area to hit, but also the *most* vulnerable side of the target. The **back lip** profile offers the vulnerability of the belly on profile but without as much surface area to hit.

These two profiles are the *hardest* to break.

The **edge on** profile offers the *least* amount of surface area to hit. It is not the hardest to break, however. The **dome on** profile is the hardest to break because the majority of the surface exposed is the curved shoulder which gives the target its strength.

Sporting Clays Choke Chart

Choke Constrictions — CYL .000   SKT .005   IMP CYL .010   LT MOD .015
MOD .020   IMP MOD .025   LT FULL .030   FULL .035   EXT FULL .040

Standard (108 Millimeter)

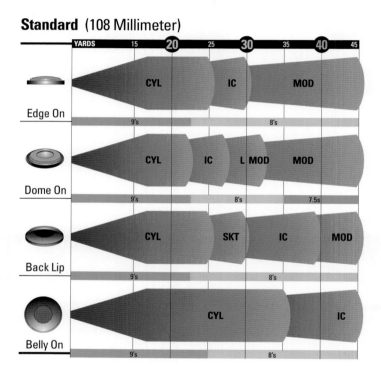

Sporting Clays Choke Chart

Choke Constrictions – CYL .000   SKT .005   IMP CYL .010   LT MOD .015
MOD .020   IMP MOD .025   LT FULL .030   FULL .035   EXT FULL .040

Midi (90 Millimeter)

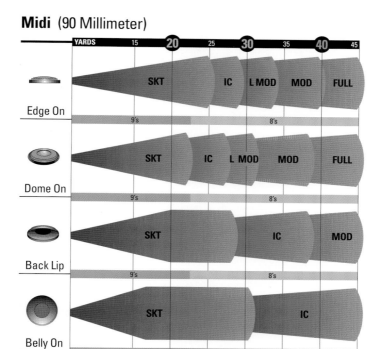

Sporting Clays Choke Chart

Choke Constrictions – CYL .000   SKT .005   IMP CYL .010   LT MOD .015
MOD .020   IMP MOD .025   LT FULL .030   FULL .035   EXT FULL .040

Rabbit

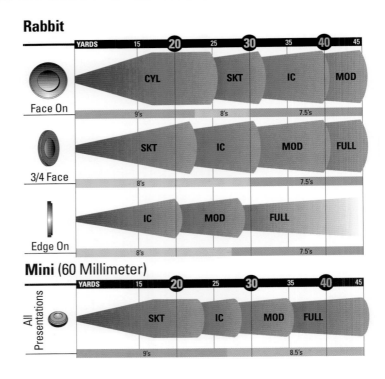

Mini (60 Millimeter)

Sporting Clays Choke Chart

Choke Constrictions – CYL .000   SKT .005   IMP CYL .010   LT MOD .015
MOD .020   IMP MOD .025   LT FULL .030   FULL .035   EXT FULL .040

Battue

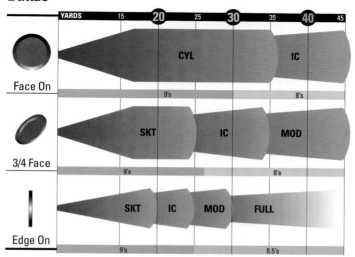

Selecting Choke and Load

1. Determine what kind of target is being thrown.
2. View target to determine which profile is being presented. Find that profile on chart.
3. Estimate distance and select choke and shot size.

Shotgun Barrels, Chokes 'n Ballistics

APPROXIMATE NUMBER OF PELLETS PER LOAD

Size	9	8	7½	6	5	4	2	BB	#4 Buck	#3 Buck	#1 Buck	#0 Buck	#00 Buck
1½				309		186	124	69			16	12	9
1¼	731	513	438	281	213	169	113	63	27		12		
1⅛	658	461	394	253	191	152	101			20			
1	585	410	350	225	170	135	90						
⅞	512	359		197	149	118							
¾	439		263	169	128	101							
½	293		175	113	85	68							

CHOKE & PATTERN PERCENTAGES

This chart shows the results to be expected as choke constriction is increased. Note the effect of choke diminishes as the upper limit of effective choke is reached.

DESIGNATION	CHOKE IN THOUSANDTHS OF AN INCH	PERCENT INCREASE OVER CYL.	PATTERN PERCENT*
Over Choke	.055"	27%	67%
Full	.040"	35%	75%
Imp. Mod.	.030"	33%	73%
Mod.	.020"	27%	67%
Imp. Cyl.	.010"	17%	57%
Skeet	.005"	13%	53%
Cyl.	0"	—	40%

*Percentages shown are averages, and individual guns or loads may show different results.

VELOCITY/ENERGY EXTERIOR BALLISTICS — SHOTGUN

Velocity (f.p.s.) at

Shot Size	f.p.s. at Muzzle	10 yds.	20 yds.	30 yds.	40 yds.	50 yds.	60 yds.
7½	1295	1070	910	795	705	630	575
8	1255	1035	880	765	675	605	550
7½	1240	1035	885	770	690	620	560
8	1235	1020	870	755	670	600	545
7½	1220	1020	875	765	680	615	560
8	1220	1010	860	750	665	595	540
7½	1200	1005	865	760	675	610	555
8	1200	995	850	745	660	590	540
9	1200	975	820	710	625	555	505
8	1165	970	835	730	650	585	530
9	1165	950	805	695	615	550	495
8	1155	965	830	725	645	580	530
9	1155	945	800	695	610	545	495
7½	1145	965	835	735	655	595	540
8	1145	960	825	720	640	580	525

Energy in ft./lbs. per pellet at

Muzzle	10 yds.	20 yds.	30 yds.	40 yds.	50 yds.	60 yds.
4.63	3.16	2.30	1.74	1.37	1.10	0.91
3.69	2.50	1.80	1.36	1.07	0.86	0.70
4.24	2.94	2.16	1.64	1.30	1.06	0.87
3.57	2.43	1.76	1.33	1.05	0.84	0.69
4.11	2.86	2.11	1.62	1.28	1.04	0.86
3.48	2.38	1.73	1.32	1.03	0.83	0.69
3.97	2.79	2.06	1.59	1.26	1.02	0.85
3.37	2.32	1.69	1.29	1.02	0.82	0.68
2.38	1.57	1.11	0.83	0.64	0.51	0.42
3.18	2.21	1.62	1.24	0.98	0.80	0.66
2.24	1.49	1.07	0.80	0.62	0.50	0.41
3.18	2.18	1.60	1.23	0.97	0.79	0.65
2.20	1.47	1.06	0.79	0.62	0.49	0.40
3.62	2.57	1.93	1.49	1.19	0.97	0.81
3.07	2.15	1.58	1.22	0.96	0.78	0.65

TIME/DROP EXTERIOR BALLISTICS — SHOTGUN

Shot Size	f.p.s. at Muzzle	Time of Flight (seconds) to						Drop (inches) at					
		10 yds.	20 yds.	30 yds.	40 yds.	50 yds.	60 yds.	10 yds.	20 yds.	30 yds.	40 yds.	50 yds.	60 yds.
7½	1295	.026	.056	.091	.132	.177	.227	0.1	0.6	1.6	3.3	6.0	9.0
8	1255	.027	.058	.095	.137	.184	.236	0.1	0.6	1.7	3.6	6.5	10.7
7½	1240	.027	.058	.094	.136	.184	.133	0.1	0.6	1.7	3.6	6.5	10.5
8	1235	.027	.059	.099	.138	.186	.238	0.1	0.7	2.1	3.7	6.6	11.0
7½	1220	.027	.059	.096	.137	.184	.235	0.1	0.7	1.8	3.6	5.6	10.2
8	1220	.027	.059	.097	.139	.187	.240	0.1	0.7	1.8	3.8	6.8	11.1
7½	1220	.027	.060	.097	.139	.186	.238	0.1	0.7	1.8	3.7	6.7	10.9
8	1200	.027	.060	.098	.141	.189	.242	0.1	0.7	1.9	3.8	6.9	11.3
9	1200	.028	.062	.101	.146	.197	.254	0.1	0.7	2.0	4.1	7.5	12.4
8	1200	.028	.062	.100	.144	.193	.247	0.2	0.7	1.9	4.0	7.2	11.8
9	1165	.029	.063	.103	.149	.201	.258	0.2	0.8	2.1	4.3	7.8	12.9
8	1165	.029	.062	.101	.145	.194	.248	0.2	0.8	2.0	4.0	7.3	11.9
9	1155	.029	.064	.104	.150	.202	.260	0.2	0.8	2.1	4.3	7.9	13.0
7½	1145	.029	.062	.101	.144	.192	.245	0.2	0.7	2.0	4.0	7.1	11.6
8	1145	.029	.063	.102	.146	.195	.250	0.2	0.8	2.1	4.1	7.4	12.0

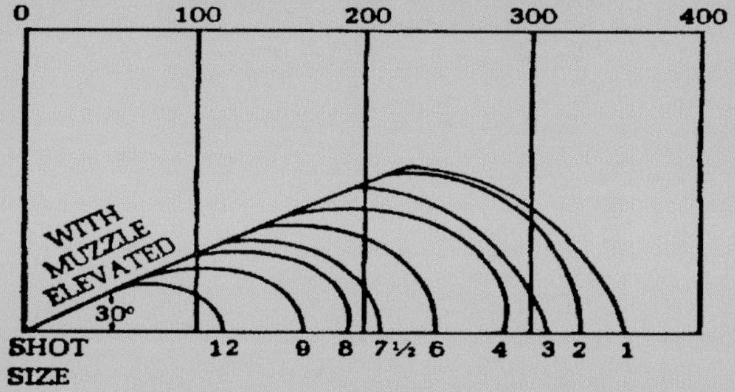

RECOIL IN FOOT/POUNDS

Gun Weight (pounds)	Gauge	Load	Comments	Recoil (ft./lbs.)
8.4	12	2¾"	1⅛ oz. shot	12.5
7.5	20	3" Mag.	factory load	13.0
6.0	12	2¾"	heavy game load	16.0
5.5	12	1 oz. slug		17.0
5.5	12	2¾"	1¼ oz. shot	24.0
5.5	12	3" Mag.	1¼ oz. slug	33.0
8.0	12	3" Mag.	1⅞ oz. shot	37.0
6.0	12	3" Mag.	1¼ oz. slug	45.0
6.25	12	3½" Mag.	2 oz. shot	55.0
6.25	12	3½" Mag.	2¼ oz. shot	70.0

RANGE OF AMERICAN SHOT

YARDS: 0, 100, 200, 300, 400

WITH MUZZLE ELEVATED 30°

SHOT SIZE: 12, 9, 8, 7½, 6, 4, 3, 2, 1

Reprinted with permission of Bruce Buck.

National Sporting Clays Association Class Punch Summary

Punches earned based on number of shooters in class

HOA: The shooter with the highest score and all ties in an event, where there is a minimum of ten (10) total shooters, shall receive a minimum of one (1) punch no matter what class the shooter is in.

Number of Entries in class	Punches earned
0–2	No punch
3–9	One (1) punch for high score and all ties
10–14	Two (2) punches for high score and all ties One (1) punch for the second highest score and all ties
15–29	Four (4) punches for high score and all ties. Two (2) punches for second highest score and all ties. One (1) punch for third highest score and all ties.
30–44	Four (4) punches for high score and all ties. Four (4) punches for second highest score and ties. Two (2) punches for third highest score and ties. One (1) punch for fourth highest score and all ties.

45+   Four (4) punches to first, second and third highest
                      scores and all ties.
                  Three (3) punches for fourth highest score and all ties.
                  Two (2) punches for fifth highest score and all ties.
                  One (1) punch for sixth highest score and all ties.

Punches required to move up in class

E Class to D Class   4 punches

D Class to C Class   6 punches

C Class to B Class   8 punches

B Class to A Class   12 punches

A Class to AA Class   14 punches

AA Class to Master Class   20 punches

Note: Punches must be earned in Shooter's current class in order for them to be used in moving up in class. A person earning more than the necessary punches to move up in class enters the new class with no punches.

Copyright 2013 NSCA Rule Book. Reprinted with permission of the NSCA.

GLOSSARY OF TERMS

adjustable comb This is when the top portion of the shotgun stock is cut out and adjustable shims are installed. It allows the shooter to raise or lower the upper portion of the stock where it contacts the shooter's face. Many adjustable combs also allow for left or right adjustment of the comb.

aftermarket chokes There are many specialty choke manufacturers, and they make chokes that will fit almost any gun. They all tout superior performance.

backbored The barrel of the gun is given a slightly larger inside diameter to help open up the shot pattern.

black powder A gunpowder that is the antecedent of the smokeless powder used today. It burns dirty and produces a large volume of smoke.

bore snake A cloth and brass rope that can be dragged through the barrel to clean it in one fell swoop.

cast The bend of the stock to the left and the right, cast "on" to the left and cast "off" to the right.

chamber The part of the barrel that holds the shotgun shell.

chokes Chokes constrict the barrel, altering the pattern of shot. The standard chokes are skeet, improved cylinder, modified, and full. Full is the tightest choke.

competition trigger A trigger that has been worked on by a professional gunsmith to make sure it breaks cleanly and has no creep or excessive take-up. It can also be adjusted to break with very little pressure from your finger. This is measured in pounds and is called trigger pull.

cylinder bore A gun that is not choked whatsoever.

dead gun This occurs when the gun is left in such an awkward position that it is difficult if not impossible to move it quickly to the next target. Lead has been established, but there is no room or no time to move the gun.

dram equivalent The velocity of the shot based on the equivalent weight of black powder.

drop at comb A measurement of the height of the front of the comb compared to the rib of the gun. 1^1/2-inch drop is typical.

drop at heel A measurement of the height of the back of the comb compared to the rib of the gun. 2^1/4-inch drop is typical.

forcing cone The transition area between the gun's chamber and barrel. A favorite aftermarket modification is to extend the length of the forcing cone. Many believe extended forcing cones give better choke and recoil performance.

gauge The number of lead balls it takes to equal one pound when placed in different diameter barrels. For example, it takes 12 balls of the same size to equal one pound when placed in a 12-gauge barrel. It takes 16 balls the same size to fit in the smaller 16-gauge barrel, 20 balls for a 20-gauge gun, and 28 for the yet smaller 28-gauge gun. The exception is the .410, which is a measure by the hundredths of the inch, more readily known to shooters as caliber.

LOP Stands for length of pull or how long the distance is from the end of the stock to the trigger.

misfire The term used to indicate the shotgun shell did not fully discharge.

muzzle flip The tendency for the front of the gun to rise when it is fired.

no bird The term used to indicate that the target thrown is not to be considered a legal target, i.e., broken or irregular.

over-and-under shotgun The barrels are placed one on top of the other.

patterning board A large enough board made of tough enough material to measure the pattern of the pellet charge.

pitch The angle of the recoil pad in relation to the barrel's rib.

primer The device that ignites the gunpowder.

pull/pull it The command given by a shooter for the trapper to release the bird.

recoil The felt impact of the shotgun on the shoulder and body of the shooter when it goes off.

recoil management system Various aftermarket devices that help absorb felt recoil when the gun goes off.

recoil pad A rubber, plastic, or leather cushion that is fixed to the butt of the gun to help reduce the felt impact when the gun is discharged.

rib The metal sighting plane that runs atop the barrel, punctuated with a front and sometimes middle bead.

semiautomatic A single-barrel firearm that holds multiple shells and automatically loads the next shell when one is fired. Also referred to as an autoloader.

short barrel Skeet barrels are the shortest of the various competition guns, around 28 inches. Sporting clays and trap guns can go as long as 34 inches. Tom's grouse gun, known as a NAVHDA special (North American Versatile Hunting Dog Association), has a barrel length of 20 inches. Legal barrel length minimum is 18 inches.

side-by-side shotgun The most venerable shotgun of them all, the side-by-side places the barrels right next to one another on a flat plane.

smoke ball/ink ball A perfect hit, when the target is reduced to such small pieces it appears to have gone up in smoke.

standard target A round, orange pitch target measuring 108 millimeters in diameter. May sometimes be colored green or black.

trigger pull The weight in pounds that it takes to make the trigger fire.

wad The plastic or paper cup that holds the shot charge. The wad separates the gunpowder from the shot charge.

ACKNOWLEDGMENTS

The authors would like to thank the following people for their aid and encouragement in the writing of this book: Lisa Levinson and Marlene Brannon, for putting up with endless conversations about sporting clays, shotguns, targets, and ammo, to the exclusion of all else. Lt. Col. George Philip, USMC Ret., for his perfect shooting form, which made him an ideal model for many of the photographs in this book. Henry Trial and Earle Glidden, for setting the most varied and challenging sporting clays courses in Maine. Sarah St. Pierre, for her endless good humor and enthusiasm for the sport. Jim McMullen, for his unceasing efforts to make the Arnold Trail Sportsman's Association the best it can be. Keith McDonald and Chuck Willey, for their similar efforts at the L. L. Bean 5-stand in Freeport, Maine. George Pelletier, for making the Scarborough Fish & Game Association such a great place to shoot sporting clays. Jerald "Bub" Copp, for always being a gentleman, friend, and great shooting partner. Buzz Mendoza, a champion shooter, for his expert tutorials and all-around help. Anthony Matarese Jr., for his invaluable assistance in preparing this book. Judith Schnell, for her expert publishing acumen. Bruce Buck, a very knowledgeable man, for his invaluable assistance. Gil Ash, a true gentleman and one of sporting clays' greatest coaches and philosophers, for his generous nature and his gracious assistance. Chris and Audrey Maest, of Clay Target Sports, and Todd Beinhauer, for their professionalism and expertise.

INDEX

Page numbers in italics indicate illustrations, sidebars, tables and charts.